SECURE
IN
CHRIST

Dr. Cathy Burns

Sharing
212 E. 7th St. (C)
Mt. Carmel, PA 17851-2211

570- 339 - 2211

Mother
Jean Burns

TABLE OF CONTENTS

Chapter One

SECURE IN CHRIST

Some questions that have plagued mankind for millennia is "Where am I going when I die?" and "How can I be sure of heaven?" Most people hope that they will go to heaven but they really don't know for sure. They believe that if their good deeds outweigh their bad deeds, then they will get to heaven. Many religions teach various kinds of rituals or say that works are necessary to earn one's way to heaven. Some teach that everyone is going to heaven regardless of the way they live. Others insist that to reach heaven, one must be a member of a particular church. Still others claim that a state of perfection is only reached through reincarnation. Yet others contend that there is no heaven at all.

Of course, our answer to this perplexing inquiry is answered by the Bible. Jesus said: "Ye shall know the truth, and the truth shall make you free" (John 8:32). He also said: "I am the way, the truth, and the life: no man cometh unto the Father, but by Me" (John 14:6). John 17:17 says: "Thy word is truth."

It is through God's Word that we can find the truth and know that we are assured of going to heaven when we die. The Bible clearly sets forth the guidelines for us to follow and then gives us the assurance that we can know **for sure** that we are saved. I John 5:13 says: "These things have I written unto you that believe on the name of the Son of God; that ye may **KNOW** that ye have eternal life, and that ye may believe on the name of the Son of God." "And this is the record, that God hath given to us eternal life, and **THIS LIFE IS IN HIS SON"** (I John 5:11). "He that hath the Son hath life; and he that hath not the Son of God hath not life" (I John 5:12).

Having assurance of one's salvation is a comforting fact. We can truly be secure in Christ. We can rest on His promises and know that His protecting hand is there to lead us. We can feel His presence and realize that He will guide us into all truth (John 16:13). We do not have to continually worry and wonder if we are ready or fit for heaven. We can know **FOR SURE** that we are saved and that we are the children of God (John 1:12).

The purpose of this book is to help you to determine if you are ready for heaven and if you are really, truly secure in Christ. Are you living the kind of life that the Bible tells us we must live? To be able to rest secure in Christ, we must take His precious Word and apply it to our hearts and lives. "If we walk in the light, as He is in the light, we have fellowship one with another, and the blood of Jesus Christ His Son cleanseth us from all sin" (I John 1:7).

EXAMINE YOURSELVES

II Corinthians 13:5 tells us: **"EXAMINE** yourselves, whether ye be in the faith; **PROVE** your own selves." The verses given throughout this book will help you to examine and prove yourselves in light of God's Word. We must remember that we cannot make the Bible fit our lifestyle but we must align our lifestyle to fit with the Bible. Obeying God's Word will bring this security and peace of mind that so many people are looking and searching for.

The Bible clearly tells us that **ALL** have sinned, and come short of the glory of God" (Romans 3:23). Because of sin, **ALL** are separated from God because God is a holy God and cannot look upon sin. Habakkuk 1:13 says that God is "of purer eyes than to behold evil, and canst not look on iniquity." Because of this, we needed someone to bridge the gap between mankind and God. Jesus was the only person who was able to do this. I Timothy 2:5 explains that: "There is one God, and one mediator between God and men, the man Christ Jesus."

Christ came "not to call the righteous, but sinners to repentance" (Luke 5:32; Mark 2:17; Matthew 9:13). He died that He might redeem us from our sins and that through His sacrifice on Calvary, we could be made holy. It is through Christ's death and resurrection that we are able to go to heaven, but ONLY those who accept Christ's atonement have this privilege. "As many as received Him, to them gave He power to become the sons of God, even to them that believe on His name" (John 1:12).

After we accept Christ, we can have the blessed assurance that our sins are forgiven and that we are on our way to heaven. "Therefore if any man be in Christ, he is a new creature: old things are passed away; behold, all things are become new" (II Corinthians 5:17). We are no longer under Satan's control. Our old sinful ways and appetites are done away with. We have a new and fresh desire to please our new Master, who is Christ. We have a longing to do what is righteous and just. We will not feel comfortable doing something that is sinful as we do not want to hurt Christ, the One who gave His life for us in our behalf.

If you claim to be a Christian and do not have a desire to serve and **OBEY** Christ, I strongly suggest that you **"EXAMINE YOURSELF"** as Peter tells us to do. There is a good possibility that you really were not saved when you thought you were. If you are living the same sinful way as you lived before you came to Christ, you have not been born again or saved.

You may have made a **PROFESSION** with your mouth but you never received the **POSSESSION** of eternal life. When anyone truly comes to Christ, there will be a difference in his or her life. It is true that people who have lived a moral and decent life (as much as is possible without Christ) prior to their salvation or conversion experience, will not have as big of a change in their lives as those who are adulterers, murderers, blasphemers, drunkards, etc., but there will still be a change of the heart which will impact your life in some way. If you have not had this change of heart, you are not in Christ.

However, there are some who have truly been born again. They have experienced a changed life but after a while they fall back into their old habits or sinful ways. These are the ones who have the most doubt about their salvation. Many of them have guilty consciences and they continually question their pastor, radio talk show hosts, or friends if they are still saved. In most cases, they are assured that even in this sinful and vile condition, they will go to heaven because "once a son, always a son." Actually, those who are truly in Christ need not ask others if they are saved for they would be enjoying the fellowship with Christ and have the assurance of salvation.

FINAL AUTHORITY

This book is written especially for those who question their salvation so that they will be able to see from the Bible if they are still really saved or not. This book is to help them to be able to know **FOR SURE** if they are secure in Christ. We must remember that we will be judged by the Word of God, and, therefore, this must be our **FINAL AUTHORITY** and source. We cannot rely on man's word. We won't be able to stand before God on judgment day and say: "So-and-so said that even though I was living in sin, I still was saved," for God has given us His Word and it's His Word that counts, not the word or ideas of any Bible professor, Bible teacher, or Dr. so-and-so.

Many who will be reading this book already have preconceived ideas about this issue. They have heard numerous sermons, radio and TV programs, etc., giving this viewpoint, but John 5:39 commands us: **"SEARCH THE SCRIPTURES; for in them ye THINK ye have eternal life: and they are they which testify of Me."** **THIS IS THE MOST IMPORTANT ISSUE** anyone will ever face—the eternal destiny of one's soul. Your decision made here on earth will affect you for all eternity. A wrong choice made here on earth cannot be corrected when you stand before God. Pleading ignorance or incorrect advice will do no good. **YOU** are responsible for your decision and it had better be based on God's Word because that is the standard by which we will be judged. Please set aside your preconceived notions and ask the Lord Himself to reveal to you His Word. Ask Him to show you the truth of His Word. Bow your head right now and pray for His guidance. Ask Him to open your eyes to see what His Word teaches. Don't take my word for it, but get out your Bibles and check out the verses for yourself. "For the **word of God** is quick, and powerful, and sharper than any twoedged sword, piercing even to the dividing asunder of soul and spirit, and of the joints and marrow, and is a discerner of the thoughts and intents of the heart" (Hebrew 4:12). We will now begin our search of the Scriptures, for Jesus said: "The word that I have spoken, the same shall judge him in the last day" (John 12:48).

Chapter Two

ONCE A SON, ALWAYS A SON?

One phrase that is repeated quite frequently is "once a son, always a son." We are told that once we become a son of God, we can never lose our sonship. There is nothing that we can do—blasphemy, murder, adultery, lying, etc.—that will ever make us lose our sonship status. We are then told that once you are born you cannot be unborn. It is also stated that your earthly father would not disown a rebellious son, so God will never disown you even though you sin grievously and willfully. Is this what the Bible teaches?

Isaiah 1:18 says: "Come now, and **let us reason together, saith the Lord**," so let us be reasonable and see what the Bible really does say. First of all, we cannot always compare the natural things with the things of God for they will not always fit. In fact, Paul says in I Corinthians 2:13: "Which things also we speak, not in the words which man's wisdom teacheth, but which the Holy Ghost teacheth; **COMPARING SPIRITUAL THINGS WITH SPIRITUAL.**" We really cannot compare our earthly sonship with our heavenly sonship. We have no choice in choosing who our earthly parents are and we have no choice in being born. However, we do have a choice to come to God: **"Choose** you this day whom ye will serve" (Joshua 24:15).

In the natural sense, once a person is circumcised, he will remain circumcised. However, <u>spiritually</u> speaking, we find a different situation. Romans 2:25 states: "Circumcision verily profiteth, if thou keep the law: but if thou be a breaker of the law, **thy circumcision is made uncircumcision.**" This is obviously referring to a spiritual circumcision (of the heart). We cannot look at the Scriptures with the eyes of a natural man, for I Corinthians 2:14 reminds us that **"the natural man receiveth not the things of the Spirit of God:** for they are foolishness unto him: neither can he know them, because they are spiritually discerned."

Remember, we are **ADOPTED** into God's family (Galatians 4:5; Ephesians 1:5; Romans 8:15, 8:23, 9:4). This means that we had **another** father before coming to Christ. (Even in the natural sense, when a person is adopted, it means that there was **another** father previously.) Since we are all born in sin (Romans 3:23; Galatians 3:22), our first father would have been Satan as John 8:44 tells us: "Ye are of your father the devil, and the lusts of your father ye will do." So, logically, applying the phrase, "once a son, always a son" to this situation would mean that we are sons of Satan and therefore, "once a son, always a son." This would leave us **NO HOPE of EVER** being saved because "once a son, **ALWAYS** a son."

However, we know that if we repent of our sins and come to Christ, we can **"BECOME** the sons of God" (John 1:12). Now, since we are able to change our sonship status from a son of Satan to a son of God, then the phrase "once a son, always a son" is not true. Also, if this status can be changed one time, then it can be changed again.

Of course, logic alone will not suffice. Something may seem logical but if it isn't backed up by God's Word, then it may not really be logical after all, so let's see what the Bible teaches about this issue of sonship.

In Luke 15:11-32 we have the perfect example—especially since Jesus Himself gives it. It reads (in part):

A certain man had two sons: And the younger of them said to his father, Father, give me the portion of goods that falleth to me. And he divided unto them his living. And not many days after the younger son gathered all together, and took his journey into a far country, and there **wasted his substance with riotous living.** And when he had spent all, there arose a mighty famine in that land; and he began to be in want. And he went and joined himself to a citizen of that country; and he sent him into his fields to feed swine. And he would fain have filled his belly with the husks that the swine did eat: and no man gave unto him. And when he came to himself, he said, How many hired servants of my father's have bread enough and to spare, and I perish with hunger! **I will arise and go to my father,** and will say unto him, Father, I have sinned against heaven, and before thee, And am no more worthy to be called thy son: make me as one of thy hired servants. And he arose, and came to his father. But when he was yet a great way off, his **father saw him, and had compassion,** and ran, and fell on his neck, and kissed him. And the son said unto him, **Father, I have sinned against heaven, and in thy sight, and am no more worthy to be called thy son.** But the father said to his servants, Bring forth the best robe, and put it on him; and put a ring on his hand, and shoes on his feet: And bring hither the fatted calf, and kill it; and let us eat, and be merry.

There are several things that must be noted about this situation. The boy was in his father's house. He was secure there but he himself went into a far country. His sinful lifestyle led him to leave the father—the father did not leave him. After a time of this sinful living, he realized how foolish he was, so he decided to **RETURN** to the father. The father was at the same place all the time, but it was the son's transgressions that separated them. Isaiah 59:2 says: "Your iniquities have **separated** between you and your God, and **your sins have hid His**

face from you, that He will not hear." Also, "If I regard iniquity in my heart, the Lord will not hear me" (Psalm 66:18).

In Isaiah 50:1 God asked: "Where is the bill of your mother's divorcement, whom I have put away? or which of My creditors is it to whom I have sold you? Behold, **FOR YOUR INIQUITIES HAVE YE *SOLD YOURSELVES,*** and for your transgressions is your mother put away." Our sins will **ALWAYS** separate us from God and while we are in a sinful condition, we are no longer God's child.

Now, when the prodigal son did return home, we notice that he also confessed his wrongdoing. I John 1:9 says: "**IF** we **CONFESS** our sins, He is faithful and just to forgive us our sins, and to cleanse us from all unrighteousness." Christ's forgiveness for our sins is attained through our confession. If we do not confess, we are not forgiven. "He that covereth his sins shall not prosper: but whoso **CONFESSETH** *AND FOR-SAKETH* them shall have mercy" (Proverbs 28:13). The father of the prodigal son was ready and waiting for his son's return— but it was up to the son to come back home and it was also up to the son to confess.

DEAD AND ALIVE AGAIN

After the son had returned home and confessed, the father received him, but the most important part is what the father says in Luke 15:24: "For this my son **WAS DEAD, AND IS ALIVE** *AGAIN;* **HE WAS LOST, AND IS FOUND.** Now in the natural sense, the boy was not dead, so we know that this is referring to the spiritual sense. The boy, **while living in sin, was** lost, but **after** confession and repentance, is once again found. Remember also, JESUS is the one giving this example and HE said that the boy was dead, but is alive **AGAIN.** In fact, this part is so important, that this explanation is **REPEATED** in Luke 15:32: "It was meet that we should make

merry, and be glad: for this thy brother **was dead, and is alive
again; and was lost, and is found."**

This is not the only example that Jesus gave. Right before
this lesson of the prodigal son, Jesus told about a lost coin:

Either what woman having ten pieces of silver, if
she lose one piece, doth not light a candle, and sweep
the house, and seek diligently till she find it? And when
she hath found it, she calleth her friends and her neighbours together, saying, Rejoice with me; for I have found
the piece which I had lost. **Likewise,** I say unto you,
**there is joy in the presence of the angels of God
over one SINNER that repenteth.** (Luke 15:8-10)

To make sure that the point is understood, Jesus gave a
third parable in this same chapter.

What man of you, having an hundred sheep, if
he lose one of them, doth not leave the ninety and nine
in the wilderness, and go after that **which is lost,** until
he find it? And when he hath found it, he layeth it on
his shoulders, rejoicing. And when he cometh home,
he calleth together his friends and neighbours, saying
unto them, Rejoice with me; for I have found my sheep
which was lost. (Luke 15:4-6)

Again, there are some things that need to be noticed in
this parable. There are 100 sheep in the fold. One wanders
away from the fold and the shepherd goes looking for it. The
sheep that left the fold is referred to as **"LOST."** Then Jesus
adds: " I say unto you, that **LIKEWISE** joy shall be in heaven
over one **SINNER** that repenteth, more than over ninety and
nine just persons, which need no repentance" (Luke 15:7). Can
you see that the sheep that was **IN THE FOLD** and **WAN-
DERED OFF,** is not only called **"lost"** but also a **"sinner."**

There is an interesting comment along with this parable in Matthew 18:12-14:

> How think ye? if a man have an hundred sheep, and one of them be gone astray, doth he not leave the ninety and nine, and goeth into the mountains, and seeketh that which is gone astray? And <u>if so be that he find it</u>, verily I say unto you, he rejoiceth more of that sheep, than of the ninety and nine which went not astray. Even so it is not the will of your Father which is in heaven, that one of these little ones <u>should perish</u>.

Did you notice that this passage says **"IF SO BE THAT HE FIND IT?"** The implication is that the sheep MAY NOT BE FOUND AGAIN OR MAY NOT COME BACK TO THE FOLD! Once the sheep leaves the fold, there is not a 100% guarantee that the sheep will come back. There is a hope that he will return, and God certainly does not want ANY ONE to perish (II Peter 3:9), but we have to realize that when the sheep, the coin, and the prodigal son were away from the father's house, they were referred to as "lost," "sinner," and "dead." While in this lost state, they were not considered as a son or part of the fold. "Once a son, always a son?" No, not according to the Bible.

ONCE IS ENOUGH

I cannot find **ONE** verse that says that I can commit sin and still be assured of going to heaven (and I've read the Bible through cover to cover 23 times). Furthermore, a Scriptural principle only needs to be mentioned **ONE** time for it to be valid. If every verse I've listed said the same thing, the Bible would be extremely redundant. Certain principles are laid out and then the rest of the Scriptures fall into place. The same thing does not need to be repeated over and over and over again to be valid. The word "Lucifer" is only mentioned in Isaiah 14:12, but this one verse tells us about this angelic being who fell from heaven. Other verses harmonize with this passage but the name "Lucifer" is to be found nowhere else. "All have sinned, and come short of the glory of God" (Romans 3:23) is only listed one time but this verse is used over and over again in our witnessing to sinners. Satan said unto Eve: "Ye shall not surely die" (Genesis 3:4). This is only listed one time. Just because other Scriptures do not repeat this, does not invalidate that Satan said it.

We are only told ONE time: "And as it is appointed unto men once to die, but after this the judgment" (Hebrews 9:27), but this is sufficient for us to believe this statement and base our doctrine upon it. Every statement, condition, stipulation, etc., cannot be reiterated in every verse or even every chapter or book. We know that all have sinned (Romans 3:23; 5:12) and that whosoever does not believe is damned (Mark 16:16; John 3:18, 36), etc. All the Scriptures must correlate and must be taken together. When this is done we have a whole and complete picture.

What is amazing, however, is that the Bible lists **hundreds upon hundreds of verses** that reiterate that a child of God cannot live in sin and still be a child of God. Certainly, God was trying to give us every possible warning that He could to show us that we need a holy life to be able to please Him and to get to heaven. If sin could enter heaven, then the death of His only begotten Son, Jesus Christ, would have been unnecessary. Sin cannot enter heaven: "And there shall **in no wise** enter into it **any thing that defileth,** neither whatsoever worketh abomination, or maketh a lie: but they which are written in the Lamb's book of life" (Revelation 21:27). Our body is the temple of God and if we defile it by commiting sin, we are lost and cannot enter heaven. "If any man **defile** the temple of God, him shall God destroy; for the temple of God is holy, which temple ye are" (I Corinthians 3:17).

Chapter Three

NO MAN CAN PLUCK THEM OUT OF MY HAND

One passage of Scripture that is used over and over again is John 10:28-29: "I give unto them eternal life; and they shall never perish, neither shall any man pluck them out of My hand. My Father, which gave them Me, is greater than all; and no man is able to pluck them out of My Father's hand." Of course, this verse is true. No one can pluck us out of Christ's hand but as mentioned in the previous chapter, an individual can walk away from the fold. As also mentioned, our iniquities separate us from God (Isaiah 59:2).

This passage, however, says more than most people ever point out. Just the verse before this we find: "My sheep hear My voice, and I know them, and they follow Me" (John 10:27). Here is the secret to being secure in Christ and that is **FOL-LOWING** Him. It is clear that those people (sheep) who follow Christ are the ones who will not be plucked out of Christ's hand, but those who **FOLLOW** Christ are the **ONLY** ones who are secure within the Father's hand. Notice also verse 5: "And a stranger will they not follow, but will flee from him: for they know not the voice of strangers." A child in a home can be secure behind a locked door. No one can enter but if the child unlocks the door, he can walk out and follow a stranger. If you start to follow a stranger, you are no longer secure within the Father's hand.

After verse 27 comes verse 28 which starts: "I give unto them eternal life." Unto whom? The answer is unto those who **FOLLOW** Christ. It is quite simple to see what is being taught here when we take the Scriptures as they are. If we are not following Christ, then we are not promised eternal life. This eternal life is only promised to those who follow Christ. We are not following Christ when we are sidetracked into following a stranger.

A CONTINUAL PROCESS

Another point of interest is that the words "follow" and "hear" are in the present tense in Greek. The present tense is a little different in Greek than in English. The Greek present tense means a **CONTINUAL** process—something that is started now and **continues** on into the future. So, when John 10 says that Christ's sheep hear His voice and follow Him, it simply means that Christians are **CONTINUALLY** following and obeying His commands.

The King James Version conveys the Greek present tense by adding "eth" to many of the words that are in the present tense such as "abideth," "dwelleth," "remaineth," "believeth," etc. Whenever (at least in most cases) a word ends in "eth" you can know that the present, continual tense is being referred to. When you read your Bible, keep this in mind for it is **very important** in understanding what is being indicated. This knowledge can help you comprehend more of the Scriptures. For instance, in John 3:16 we find: "For God so loved the world, that He gave His only begotten Son, that whosoever **BELIEVETH** in Him should not perish, but have everlasting life." The word "believeth" is once again in the present tense, so this verse, in essence, says: "Whosoever believes now and **CONTINUES** to believe in the future, should not perish, but have everlasting life." The condition of eternal life is based on a continual believing.

Of course, those who believe that a person cannot lose his or her salvation, will say that eternal life is a free gift and once God has given us a free gift, He will not take it away from us. What does the Bible teach about this? First of all, God is not taking our free gift away. This gift was given on condition and if the condition is not met, the gift is forfeited. Second, Jesus Himself is eternal life as I John 5:11-12 reveals: "This is the record, that God hath given to us eternal life, and **THIS LIFE IS IN HIS SON**. He that hath the Son hath life; and he that hath not the Son of God hath not life." "This is life eternal, that they might know Thee the only true God, and Jesus Christ, whom Thou hast sent" (John 17:3).

Many people teach that when we are committing willful sins, we are only out of fellowship but still a son. However I John 1:3 tells us that "our fellowship is with the Father, and with His Son Jesus Christ" and I Corinthians 1:9 states: "God is faithful, by whom ye were called unto the fellowship of His Son Jesus Christ our Lord." In other words, if we are out of fellowship, we are out of Christ, and since Christ is our eternal life, we are out of our eternal life.

FORFEITING OUR RIGHT

For an example, let's say you were given a diamond as a free gift with no strings attached. What happens if, through carelessness and negligence, you lose the diamond? Does the diamond cease to exist? Is the diamond any less valuable than it was before you lost it? Does the quality of the diamond change? Was the diamond taken out of your hand? Of course not. The **ONLY** thing that has changed is **YOUR** possession of that diamond. The diamond is still a diamond—but **YOU** no longer have it in your possession. Remember, the diamond is unchanged and it is still valuable, but it's no longer **YOURS** through **neglect or carelessness.**

We could liken Christ (and eternal life) to a diamond (although we know He is far more superior than that). When you were born again, you received Christ as a free gift through faith, but if you commit sin, you will lose your eternal life. Christ has not changed, God did not take the gift away from you, and no one plucked you out of God's hand, but you have forfeited your right to that gift because of your sin. The quality of the gift has not changed. The only change is in **YOUR** possession of the gift.

Another illustration could be that you are given a house— free of charge. What happens if you refuse to pay your taxes on that home? The home would be repossessed. Your negligence would cause you to lose your possession. Hebrews 2:1-3 warns: "Therefore we ought to give the more earnest heed to the things which we have heard, lest at any time we should let them slip. For if the word spoken by angels was stedfast, and **every transgression and disobedience received a just recompence of reward; HOW SHALL WE ESCAPE, IF WE NEGLECT SO GREAT SALVATION.**"

You could also sell the home that was given to you free of charge because you may not realize the value of it. Do you realize that Esau sold his inheritance? Hebrews 12:16-17 reminds us:

Lest there be any fornicator, or profane person, as Esau, who for one morsel of meat sold his birthright. For ye know how that afterward, when he would have inherited the blessing, he was rejected: for he found no place of repentance, though he sought it carefully with tears.

Esau actually despised his birthright (Genesis 25:34). Although we can't sell our eternal life, it is an inheritance for us (see Hebrews 9:15) and it can be lost.

NO INHERITANCE

Paul, writing to the <u>Christians</u>, commands in Ephesians 5:3-7:

> But fornication, and all uncleanness, or covetousness, **LET IT NOT BE <u>ONCE</u> NAMED AMONG YOU, AS BECOMETH SAINTS;** Neither filthiness, nor foolish talking, nor jesting, which are not convenient: but rather giving of thanks. For this ye know, that no whoremonger, nor unclean person, nor covetous man, who is an idolater, **hath any inheritance** in the kingdom of Christ and of God. **Let no man deceive you with vain words:** for because of these things cometh the wrath of God upon the children of disobedience. **Be not ye therefore partakers with them.**

Also, Galatians 5:19-21:

> Now the works of the flesh are manifest, which are these; Adultery, fornication, uncleanness, lasciviousness, Idolatry, witchcraft, hatred, variance, emulations, wrath, strife, seditions, heresies, Envyings, murders, drunkenness, revellings, and such like: of the which I tell you before, as I have also told you in time past, that **they which do such things <u>shall not inherit the kingdom of God</u>.**

Additionally, I Corinthians 6:9-11:

> Know ye not that the unrighteous shall not inherit the kingdom of God? Be not deceived: neither fornicators, nor idolaters, nor adulterers, nor effeminate, nor abusers of themselves with mankind, Nor thieves, nor covetous, nor drunkards, nor revilers, nor extortioners, shall inherit the kingdom of God. And such **WERE**

some of you: but ye are washed, but ye are sanctified, but ye are justified in the name of the Lord Jesus, and by the Spirit of our God.

If Christians cannot lose their salvation, **why** did Paul write such things to them? It would have been foolish to warn them about these things **IF** they could still commit them and go to heaven. Revelation 21:7 reminds us: "He that **overcometh** shall inherit all things; and I will be his God, and he shall be My son." Turning to Hebrews 6:12-15 we find that it is through "faith and patience" that we "inherit the promises":

That ye be not slothful, but followers of them who **through faith and patience inherit the promises.** For when God made promise to Abraham, because He could swear by no greater, He sware by Himself, Saying, Surely blessing I will bless thee, and multiplying I will multiply thee. And so, *after* **he had patiently endured, he obtained the promise.**

You may respond: "But God promised us eternal life and He would never break His promise. Therefore, if we lose our eternal life, then God is a liar." God does not break His promise and that is precisely **WHY** we **WILL** lose our gift of eternal life if we are sinning. The reason is, God promised eternal life **only** to those who **OBEY** Him and if we stop obeying Him, He must be faithful to His promise, by letting us lose our eternal life.

Furthermore, God Himself said:

And at what instant I shall speak concerning a nation, and concerning a kingdom, to build and to plant it; If it do evil in my sight, that it obey not my voice, then I will repent of the good, wherewith I said I would benefit them. (Jeremiah 18:9-10)

CHRISTIANS WARNED

God has already told us what to expect and if we go against Him, then He will fulfill His promise. He also said:

At what instant I shall speak concerning a nation, and concerning a kingdom, to pluck up, and to pull down, and to destroy it; If that nation, against whom I have pronounced, turn from their evil, I will repent of the evil that I thought to do unto them. (Jeremiah 18:7-8)

He is a fair and gracious God, but He is also a God who cannot look upon evil. If we insist on sinning, then He will allow us to go our own way, for we cannot serve two masters (Matthew 6:24; Luke 16:13).

Paul, in writing to the Christians, asked them: "Know ye not, that **to whom ye yield yourselves servants to obey, his servants ye are** to whom ye obey; **whether of sin unto death, or of obedience unto righteousness?**" (Romans 6:16). These Christians were warned that if they would sin then they would die spiritually. If they were be obedient to Christ, then they would have eternal life.

The Bible is clear enough along this line but many have tried to fit the Bible to their sinful lifestyles. Many people will use just a portion of certain verses to try to "prove" their point that a person can live in sin and still go to heaven or they will give a verse and then tell you the verse doesn't really mean what it says and then give an explanation to fit their preconceived ideas. Peter warned about such people. He wrote that Paul said "some things hard to be understood, which they that are unlearned and unstable wrest [twist or contort], as they do also the other scriptures, unto their own destruction" (II Peter 3:16). We can try to make the Scriptures fit our viewpoint and our lifestyle but we can twist them unto our own destruction. When dealing with your eternal welfare and destiny, there is **no room** to take a chance and say that the Bible allows a Christian to live a sinful life and still go to heaven. It just won't work.

"I beseech you therefore, brethren, by the mercies of God, that ye present your bodies a living sacrifice, **HOLY, ACCEPT-ABLE UNTO GOD,** which is your **reasonable** service" (Romans 12:1). "As **He which hath called you is holy, <u>so be ye holy</u>** in all manner of conversation; Because it is written, **Be ye holy; for I am holy**" (I Peter 1:15-16).

Chapter Four

THERE IS NOW NO CONDEMNATION

Romans 8:1 is one verse that many people use to say that once we are saved we have no condemnation—no matter what sin we may commit. Let's look at this verse: "There is therefore now no condemnation to them which are in Christ Jesus" (Romans 8:1a). I can say, "Praise the Lord" to that. As Christians we do not have condemnation knowing that our past has been forgiven. We do not have to carry guilt over our sinful past since it has all been cleansed by Christ's atonement on Calvary. This assurance, however, only applies to those **"who walk not after the flesh, but after the Spirit"** (Romans 8:1b). This part of the verse never seems to be emphasized.

Of course, there's even more explanation in the following verses. For example, look at Romans 8:5-9:

> For they that are after the flesh do mind the things of the flesh; but they that are after the Spirit the things of the Spirit. **For to be carnally minded is death;** but to be spiritually minded is life and peace. Because **the carnal mind is enmity against God:** for it is not subject to the law of God, neither indeed can be. So then ***THEY THAT ARE IN THE FLESH CANNOT PLEASE GOD.*** But ye are not in the flesh, but in the Spirit, **IF SO BE** that the Spirit of God dwell in you. Now if any man have not the Spirit of Christ, he is none of his.

The verses are really self-explanatory. There's no need to try to read anything into them. It simply states that a Christian cannot live according to the flesh and still be a child of God. If a person is carnally minded or sinning, he is spiritually dead. Romans 8:12-14 goes even further:

> Therefore, **BRETHREN,** we are debtors, not to the flesh, to live after the flesh. **FOR IF YE LIVE AFTER THE FLESH, YE SHALL DIE:** but **IF** ye through the Spirit do mortify the deeds of the body, **ye shall live.** For **as many as are led by the Spirit of God, they are the sons of God.**

IF WE FAINT NOT

Some may try to twist the above passage to say that the death being referred to is not a spiritual death but only a physical death, but this cannot be the case because those who follow the Spirit shall live. If this refers only to physical life, then these people will never die—they'll live here on earth forever. Of course, we know this is not true, but this is the extreme some people go to in order to try to justify their own sinful lifestyle. Galatians 5:16-17: says: "Walk in the Spirit, and ye shall not fulfil the lust of the flesh. For the flesh lusteth against the Spirit, and the Spirit against the flesh: and these are contrary the one to the other."

Galatians 5:24-25 (again speaking to **CHRISTIANS)** says: "They that are Christ's have **crucified the flesh** with the affections and lusts. If we live in the Spirit, let us also walk in the Spirit."

> Be not deceived; God is not mocked: for **whatsoever a man soweth, that shall he also reap. For he that soweth to his flesh shall** of the flesh **reap corruption; but he that soweth to the Spirit shall**

of the Spirit reap *life everlasting.* And let us not be weary in well doing: for **in due season we shall reap, IF we faint not.** (Galatians 6:7-9).

Did you notice the **CONDITIONS** for reaping eternal life? We can only reap eternal life **IF we sow to the Spirit AND IF we faint not.**

Again, it is very definite that this passage is referring to **spiritual** life and death—not **physical** life and death.

Now that we can clearly see that a Christian cannot live after the flesh and still be a child of God, let's see what the Bible tells us are the sins of the flesh.

Now the works of the flesh are manifest, which are these; Adultery, fornication, uncleanness, lasciviousness, Idolatry, witchcraft, hatred, variance, emulations, wrath, strife, seditions, heresies, Envyings, murders, drunkenness, revellings, and such like: of the which I tell you before, as I have also told you in time past, that **they which do such things shall not inherit the kingdom of God.** (Galatians 5:19-21)

Mortify therefore your members which are upon the earth; fornication, uncleanness, inordinate affection, evil concupiscence, and covetousness, which is idolatry: For which things' sake the wrath of God cometh on the children of disobedience. (Colossians 3:5-6)

But now ye also put off all these; anger, wrath, malice, blasphemy, filthy communication out of your mouth. Lie not one to another, seeing that ye have put off the old man with his deeds. (Colossians 3:8-9)

After we put off the sins of the flesh, we are told what needs to be put on.

Put on therefore, as the elect of God, holy and beloved, bowels of mercies, kindness, humbleness of mind, meekness, longsuffering; Forbearing one another, and forgiving one another, if any man have a quarrel against any: even as Christ forgave you, so also do ye. And above all these things put on charity, which is the bond of perfectness. And let the peace of God rule in your hearts, to the which also ye are called in one body; and be ye thankful. Let the word of Christ dwell in you richly in all wisdom; teaching and admonishing one another in psalms and hymns and spiritual songs, singing with grace in your hearts to the Lord. And **whatsoever ye do in word or deed, do all in the name of the Lord Jesus,** giving thanks to God and the Father by Him. (Colossians 3:12-17)

John also tells us:

Love not the world, neither the things that are in the world. **If any man love the world, the love of the Father is not in him.** For all that is in the world, the lust of the flesh, and the lust of the eyes, and the pride of life, is not of the Father, but is of the world. And the world passeth away, and the lust thereof: but **HE THAT <u>DOETH</u> THE WILL OF GOD <u>ABIDETH</u> FOR EVER.** (I John 2:15-17)

Once again we see that **ONLY** those who do the will of God "abideth for ever." **These** are the people who have eternal life.

Ye adulterers and adulteresses, know ye not that the **friendship of the world is enmity with God? <u>whosoever therefore will be a friend of the world is the enemy of God.</u>** Do ye think that the scripture saith in vain, The spirit that dwelleth in us lusteth to envy? But He giveth more grace. Wherefore He saith, God resisteth the proud, but giveth grace unto the humble. Submit yourselves therefore to God. Resist the devil, and he will flee from you. Draw nigh to God, and He will draw nigh to you. Cleanse your hands, ye sinners; and purify your hearts, ye double minded. (James 4:4-8)

Do you want to be secure in Christ? If so, then you must do God's will and follow His commands. **AS LONG AS** you do so, you have perfect security. Peter tells us more about this security:

> And beside this, giving all diligence, <u>add to your faith</u> virtue; and to virtue knowledge; And to knowledge temperance; and to temperance patience; and to patience godliness; And to godliness brotherly kindness; and to brotherly kindness charity. For **IF** these things be in you, <u>and abound,</u> they make you that **ye shall neither be barren nor unfruitful** in the knowledge of our Lord Jesus Christ....Wherefore the rather, brethren, **GIVE DILIGENCE TO MAKE YOUR CALLING AND ELECTION SURE:** for **IF ye do these things, YE SHALL NEVER FALL:** For so an entrance shall be ministered unto you abundantly into the everlasting kingdom of our Lord and Saviour Jesus Christ. (II Peter 1:5-8, 10-11)

Paul, too, said that "we should bring forth fruit unto God" (Romans 7:4) and Jesus Himself said: "Ye have not chosen Me, but I have chosen you, and **ORDAINED YOU, THAT YE SHOULD GO AND BRING FORTH FRUIT,** and that your **FRUIT SHOULD REMAIN**" (John 15:16). As Christians we need to bear fruit or we cannot remain as Christ's disciples, for Jesus also said: "Herein is My Father glorified, that ye **bear much fruit; so shall ye be My disciples**" (John 15:8).

Chapter Five

YE ARE THE BRANCHES

"I am the vine, ye are the branches: He that abideth in Me, and I in him, the same bringeth forth much fruit: for without Me ye can do nothing. If a man abide not in Me, he is cast forth as a branch, and is withered; and men gather them, and cast them into the fire, and they are burned" (John 15:5-6). This passage is frequently used (or should I say, misused) to teach that we are the branches and if we do not bear fruit ("works"), then our works are burned up, but what does the Bible **REALLY** mean?

What the Bible **REALLY** means is <u>just</u> what it <u>says</u>. It clearly states that Jesus is the vine and His followers (the Christians) are the branches. Jesus adds: "IF A MAN [not his works] **ABIDE NOT** IN ME, **HE** [not his works] is **cast forth** as a branch, and is withered; and men gather them, and cast them [the BRANCHES, not the works] into the fire, and they [the BRANCHES, not the works] are burned." You can see that Jesus was differentiating between the branch and the fruit that was borne on that branch. If we do not continue to abide in Christ, our destiny is the lake of fire (unless we repent and confess our sins). The word "abide" means "continue," "stand," "tarry," "dwell," "endure," and "remain." In the Greek it means to **"stay in a given place, state, relation,** or expectancy." Also, we are secure in Christ **AS LONG AS** we remain in Him.

Observe that it is up to the individual to do the abiding. Jesus said "IF a man abide not in Me...." No one will pluck us out of the Father's hand, but we ourselves do have a choice to abide in Christ or not to abide in Christ.

It is interesting to note that when Lucifer fell from heaven, it said that he was "cast out of [his] grave like an **abominable branch**" (Isaiah 14:19). We know that his destiny is hell and those who do not remain in Christ, will be likewise cast into hell.

Returning to John 15, let's notice further: **"Every branch in Me that beareth not fruit He taketh away:** and every branch that beareth fruit, He purgeth it, that it may bring forth more fruit" (John 15:2). It is obvious that the branch is the Christian (for Jesus Himself said so) and if the branch does not bear fruit, then it is taken away. How can you take away the fruit on the branch if there is no fruit there? Obviously, you can't. Furthermore, if we bear fruit, then we are purged in order to bring forth even more fruit.

ABIDE IN ME

Jesus continues:

Abide in Me, and I in you. As the branch cannot bear fruit of itself, except it abide in the vine; no more can ye, except ye abide in Me. I am the vine, ye are the branches: He that abideth in Me, and I in him, the same bringeth forth much fruit: for without Me ye can do nothing. (John 15:4-5)

Stated simply, we must **CONTINUE** to remain in the vine to be able to bring forth fruit. If we don't bring forth fruit, then we are no longer connected to the vine (Christ). Remember that Christ is our eternal life (I John 5:11). If we lose our connection to Him, we have lost our eternal life and will be cast into the fire (unless we repent). "And let ours also LEARN TO MAINTAIN GOOD WORKS FOR NECESSARY USES, THAT THEY BE NOT UNFRUITFUL" (Titus 3:14). Our works are our fruits. "That ye might walk worthy of the Lord unto all pleasing, being FRUITFUL IN EVERY GOOD WORK, and increasing in the knowledge of God" (Colossians 1:10).

In this same discourse in John 15, Jesus states:

> As the Father hath loved Me, so have I loved you: **continue** ye in My love. **IF ye keep My commandments, ye shall abide in My love;** even as I have kept My Father's commandments, and abide in His love. These things have I spoken unto you, that My **joy might <u>remain</u> in you**, and that your joy might be full....**Ye are My friends, IF ye do whatsoever I command you.** (John 15:9-11, 14)

There is no greater authority than Christ to tell us how to live and what we must do to keep our eternal life. If Jesus points out that we can only abide in Him **as** we obey Him, then who are we to try to contend that the Bible says something different? There is no need whatsoever to read anything into this passage. It is stated clearly enough. By **changing** the word "branches" to "works" or "fruits" takes away from the clear teaching of these verses and twists the Scriptures to teach something that is not implied at all. In addition, this false teaching is sending many unsuspecting souls to hell. They think they will just lose their reward but still go to heaven, but the Bible teaches no such thing. This teaching is giving people a "false security."

TWICE DEAD

There is an interesting reference in Jude. It says:

These are spots in your feasts of charity, when they feast with you, feeding themselves without fear: clouds they are without water, carried about of winds; **trees whose fruit withereth,** without fruit, **twice dead,** plucked up by the roots. (Jude 1:12)

Notice that here were trees whose fruit withered so that it was without fruit and it was **TWICE DEAD.** This would refer to a person who was originally spiritually dead as all are born in sin. This person then got saved, bore fruit for a while and then backslide. He is now unsaved, and once again spiritually dead— thus **TWICE** DEAD.

Another passage of Scripture that deals with branches is found in Romans 11:17-24:

And if some of the branches be broken off, and thou, being a wild olive tree, wert grafted in among them, and with them partakest of the root and fatness of the olive tree; Boast not against the branches. But if thou boast, thou bearest not the root, but the root thee. Thou wilt say then, The branches were broken off, that I might be grafted in. Well; because of unbelief they were broken off, and thou standest by faith. Be not highminded, but fear: For if God spared not the natural branches, **TAKE HEED** lest He also spare not thee. Behold therefore the goodness and severity of God: on them which fell, severity; but toward thee, goodness, **if thou continue** in His goodness: **otherwise** thou also shalt be cut off. And they also, if they abide not still in unbelief, shall be grafted in: for God is able to graft them in again. For if thou wert cut out of the olive tree which is wild by nature, and wert grafted contrary to nature into a good olive tree: how much more shall these, which be the natural branches, be grafted into their own olive tree?

TAKE HEED

The "natural branches" referred to here is Israel and the "wild olive tree" shows that the Gentiles were grafted into this vine. The passage shows that the **ORIGINAL** branches were broken off because of **UNBELIEF**. We are then warned not to be highminded and think that we have nothing to lose because if the **NATURAL** branches were broken off, the grafted in branches can also be broken off. It says: "For if **God spared not the natural branches, TAKE HEED lest He also spare not thee**" (Romans 11:21). This reference adds: "But toward thee, goodness, **IF THOU CONTINUE** in His goodness: **OTHERWISE** thou also shalt be cut off" (Romans 11:22). We will only be cut off **IF** we do not **continue** to follow Christ, but if we do follow Him, we have great security. Notice that the **SAME BRANCH** can **remain** on the tree **OR** be **cut off**—depending on the action taken.

Hebrews 3:14 states: "For we are made partakers of Christ, **IF we HOLD the beginning of our confidence STEDFAST UNTO THE END.**" Also, Hebrews 3:6: "Christ as a son over His own house; whose house are we, **IF WE HOLD FAST THE CONFIDENCE AND THE REJOICING OF THE HOPE FIRM UNTO THE END.**"

Chapter Six

CAN OUR NAMES BE BLOTTED OUT?

To believe we are eternally secure no matter what we do is extremely dangerous. The reason why I believe this is so, is because people can be made to feel sure of heaven even though they continue to live in sin and are really headed for hell.

First of all, I want to state that I fully agree that Christ has accomplished 100% of our salvation. I, in no way, believe in or teach a "works" doctrine for salvation. There is absolutely **NOTHING** we can add to Christ's infinite atonement. There is **NOTHING** we can **DO** to merit eternal life. We are saved by faith, and **faith ALONE.** On the other hand, we cannot expect to live in sin and still make heaven our home. We are to live a holy life. "Pure religion and undefiled before God and the Father is this...**TO KEEP HIMSELF UNSPOTTED FROM THE WORLD"** (James 1:27). "And there shall in no wise enter into it any thing that defileth...but they which are written in the Lamb's book of life" (Revelation 21:27).

Names are written into the Lamb's book of life when a person accepts Christ as his or her personal Savior, but these names can also be blotted out. For example, Moses prayed:

> Yet now, if Thou wilt forgive their sin; and if not, blot me, I pray Thee, out of Thy book which Thou hast written. And the Lord said unto Moses,

WHOSOEVER HATH SINNED AGAINST ME, HIM WILL I BLOT OUT OF MY BOOK. (Exodus 32:32-33)

Jesus said: "He that **overcometh,** the same shall be clothed in white raiment; and I will not blot out his name out of the book of life, but I will confess his name before My Father, and before His angels" (Revelation 3:5). "And if **any** man shall take away from the words of the book of this prophecy, **GOD SHALL TAKE AWAY HIS PART OUT OF THE BOOK OF LIFE, AND OUT OF THE HOLY CITY**, and from the things which are written in this book" (Revelation 22:19).

This last verse is especially clear as it states that God will not only blot out one's name but will also **take away his part out of the holy city (heaven)!** This certainly is far more serious than just losing one's reward (as many teach). We also see that those who are judged out of this book of life are judged "according to their works":

> And I saw the dead, small and great, stand before God; and the books were opened: and another book was opened, which is the book of life: and the dead were judged out of those things which were written in the books, according to their works....And whosoever was not found written in the book of life was cast into the lake of fire. (Revelation 20:12, 15)

NO SIN ENTERS HEAVEN

We cannot commit sin and still have a claim to eternal life. Ephesians 5:3-6 reminds us:

> But fornication, and all uncleanness, or covetousness, **LET IT NOT BE ONCE NAMED AMONG YOU,** as becometh saints; Neither filthiness, nor foolish talking, nor jesting, which are not convenient: but rather

giving of thanks. For this ye know, that no whore-monger, nor unclean person, nor covetous man, who is an idolater, hath **ANY** inheritance in the kingdom of Christ and of God. **LET NO MAN DECEIVE YOU WITH VAIN WORDS:** for because of these things cometh the wrath of God upon the children of disobedience. (See also I Corinthians 6:9-11 and Galatians 5:19-21.)

The Christian walk comes even closer for if we hate our brother, we are a murderer according to I John 3:15: "Whosoever hateth his brother is a murderer: and ye know that **NO MURDERER HATH ETERNAL LIFE ABIDING IN HIM.**"

Many people who claim to be Christians would not think of committing murder or adultery but many of them think nothing about telling a lie. The Bible, however, tells us that lying is a sin and that those who do lie cannot enter heaven: "But the fearful, and unbelieving, and the abominable, and murderers, and whoremongers, and sorcerers, and idolaters, and **all liars, shall have their part in the lake which burneth with fire and brimstone:** which is the second death" (Revelation 21:8). "And there shall **IN NO WISE** enter into it any thing that defileth, neither whatsoever worketh abomination, or **maketh a lie:** but they which are written in the Lamb's book of life" (Revelation 21:27).

"For without are dogs, and sorcerers, and whoremongers, and murderers, and idolaters, and whosoever loveth and **maketh a lie**" (Revelation 22:15). "Wherefore **putting away lying,** speak every man truth with his neighbour: for we are members one of another" (Ephesians 4:25). **"Lie not** one to another, seeing that ye have put off the old man with his deeds" (Colossians 3:9).

Let's observe another passage of Scripture. II Chronicles 15:1-2 tells us that "the Spirit of God came upon Azariah the son of Oded: And he went out to meet Asa, and said unto him, Hear ye me, Asa, and all Judah and Benjamin; **THE LORD IS WITH YOU, WHILE YE BE WITH HIM;** and if ye seek Him, He will be found of you; but **IF YE FORSAKE HIM, HE WILL FORSAKE YOU.**" It is quite obvious that **NO MAN** is plucking anyone from God's hand, but we cannot be kept safe and secure if we are committing sin. In fact, the reason Jesus came was that "He shall save His people **FROM** their sins" (Matthew 1:21) He didn't come to save them so they could continue in their sins, but to save them **FROM** their sins.

NOT OF WORKS

To reiterate: there is **NOTHING** we can add to Christ's atonement nor is there **ANYTHING** we can **DO** to **MERIT** this **FREE** gift. Ephesians 2:8-9 says: "For by grace are ye saved through faith; and that not of yourselves: it is the gift of God: **NOT OF WORKS**, lest any man should boast." The very next verse, however, is quite interesting: "For we are His workmanship, created in Christ Jesus **UNTO GOOD WORKS, WHICH GOD HATH BEFORE ORDAINED THAT WE SHOULD WALK IN THEM.**" It was foreordained of God that those who are called by His name, should walk in good works. James plainly adds:

> Yea, a man may say, Thou hast faith, and I have works: shew me thy faith without thy works, and I will shew thee my **FAITH BY MY WORKS**....But wilt thou know, O vain man, that **FAITH WITHOUT WORKS IS DEAD?**...For as the body without the spirit is dead, so faith without works is dead also. (James 2:18, 20, 26)

I Timothy 6:18-19: "That they DO GOOD, that they be rich in GOOD WORKS....Laying up in store for themselves a good foundation against the time to come, that they **MAY LAY HOLD on eternal life.**" Titus 3:8 clearly admonishes that "This is a FAITHFUL SAYING, and these things I will that thou AFFIRM CONSTANTLY, that they which have believed [past tense] in God **might BE CAREFUL TO <u>MAINTAIN</u> GOOD WORKS.**" Titus 1:16 They profess that they know God; but **IN WORKS** they deny Him." "If we deny Him, He also will deny us" (II Timothy 2:12). Peter tells us that **AFTER** we believe we should **ADD** to our faith virtue, and to virtue knowledge, and to knowledge temperance, etc. "For **IF** ye **DO** these things, **ye SHALL NEVER FALL.**"

Remember, Matthew 7:21-23 warns: "Not every one that saith unto Me, Lord, Lord, shall enter into the kingdom of heaven; but he that **DOETH** the will of My Father which is in heaven." What is the will of God? See 1 Thessalonians 4:3; 5:18; I Peter 2:15; etc. Also notice: Hebrews 10:36: "For ye have need of patience, that, **<u>AFTER</u> ye have DONE the will of God, ye might receive the promise.**"

A HOLY LIFE IS REQUIRED

The Christian walk consists of more than not PRACTIC-ING sin. It also requires living a **HOLY** life:

Whosoever abideth in Him **SINNETH NOT:** whosoever sinneth hath not seen Him, neither known Him. Little children, let no man deceive you: he that **DOETH** righteousness is righteous, even as He is righteous. <u>He that committeth sin is of the devil</u>; for the devil sinneth from the beginning. For **THIS** <u>purpose the Son of God was manifested,</u> that He might destroy the works of the devil. **WHOSOEVER IS BORN OF GOD DOTH NOT COMMIT SIN.**...<u>In this</u> the children of God are manifest, and the children of the devil: whosoever doeth not righteousness is not of God, neither he that loveth not his brother. (I John 3:6-10)

"That ye may be sincere and **WITHOUT OFFENCE TILL the day of Christ"** (Philippians 1:10). "That He might present it to Himself a glorious church, **NOT HAVING SPOT, OR WRINKLE, OR ANY SUCH THING;** but that it should be **HOLY AND WITHOUT BLEMISH"** (Ephesians 5:27). Titus 2:14: "Who gave Himself for us, that He might **REDEEM US FROM ALL INIQUITY,** and **PURIFY** unto Himself a peculiar people, zealous of good works." "Seeing then that all these things shall be dissolved, what manner of persons ought ye to be in **all holy conversation and godliness"** (II Peter 3:11). "Teaching us that, **denying ungodliness and worldly lusts, we should live soberly, righteously, and godly, IN THIS PRESENT WORLD"** (Titus 2:12).

AS LONG AS we are doing the will of God we have **NO WORRY** about losing our salvation for we are secure in Christ. "He that **DOETH** the will of God **ABIDETH FOREVER"** (I John 2:17). You won't find the phrase "eternal security" in the Bible but there is one verse that is close to this and that is in Hebrews 5:9 where we are told that Christ "became the author of eternal salvation." Of course, the verse doesn't end there. He is only the author of eternal salvation "unto all them that **OBEY** Him." We obey Him by keeping His commandments. "He that hath My commandments, and **KEEPETH** them, he it is that loveth Me" (John 14:21) and "He that loveth Me not keepeth not My sayings" (John 14:24). "His commandment **IS** life everlasting" (John 12:50). "He that **KEEPETH** His commandments **DWELLETH** in Him and He in him" (I John 3:24).

Once again notice the "eth" words which denote a **CONTINUAL process.** The ones who **continually keep** God's commands are the ones in whom He continually dwells.

Again, there is security in Christ but it is dependent upon us remaining in Him. In the next chapter, we will look at a some instances where some Bible personalities had their names **blotted out** of the book of life. "From that time many of [Jesus'] disciples **WENT BACK, and WALKED NO MORE WITH HIM**" (John 6:66). "Holding faith, and a good conscience; **which some having put away concerning faith have made shipwreck**" (I Timothy 1:19). For **some are already turned aside after Satan**" (I Timothy 5:15).

Chapter Seven

SOME EXAMPLES OF BACKSLIDING

The Bible gives numerous examples of people who have backslidden. The word "backslide" means "apostasy" or "to apostatize." Hebrews 10:38a tells us: "Now the just shall live by faith: but **IF ANY MAN DRAW BACK,** My soul shall have no pleasure in him." Those who have never been saved CAN-NOT draw back from the Lord. I cannot draw back from some place I've never been. I must be there **BEFORE** I can draw back. Therefore for a person to draw back from following Christ, he or she had to have been following Him at one time.

II Peter 2:20-22 reveals:

> For **IF** <u>after they have escaped</u> the pollutions of the world through the knowledge of the Lord and Saviour Jesus Christ, they are <u>again entangled</u> therein, and <u>overcome,</u> the <u>latter end is worse</u> with them than the beginning. For **IT HAD BEEN BETTER FOR THEM NOT TO HAVE KNOWN THE WAY OF RIGHTEOUSNESS, THAN, <u>AFTER THEY HAVE KNOWN IT, TO TURN FROM THE HOLY COMMANDMENT</u> DELIVERED UNTO THEM.** But it is happened unto them according to the true proverb, The dog is turned to his own vomit <u>again;</u> and the sow that was washed to her wallowing in the mire.

LATTER END IS WORSE

There are all kinds of explanations being propagated to try to convince us that this verse does not mean what it really says, but it quite clear that this verse is referring to a Christian who backslides. Let's notice several facts. This person had escaped the pollutions of the world through the knowledge of Christ. Notice also that this person had "known the way of righteousness" and then **TURNS** from the holy commandment. Only Christians fit this category. The sinners have not escaped the pollutions of the world. Then it goes on to state that if this person who was saved is "again entangled" and "overcome," that the latter end is worse. Now, at the beginning this person had been a sinner and headed for hell, so if the latter end is **WORSE,** it cannot possibly mean that someone who gets saved and then lives in sin will only lose his or her reward, for the latter is WORSE. If we are eternally secure, how can our latter end be worse?

Verse 22 further explains that a person who is saved and then turns away from Christ is like a dog returning to his vomit and a pig returning to the mire. Some have said that this person was never saved by commenting that the pig is still a pig. Well, a human being who gets saved is still a human being! If that person backslides and returns to sin, he or she is still a human being. Just because the pig is still a pig proves absolutely nothing. It's amazing to what extreme people will go to try to justify a sinful lifestyle, but the Bible clearly tells us that the pig was **WASHED**—it was all cleaned up—and then it **returned** to its filth, and this verse is comparing the filthy pig to a saved (or "washed") person who has returned to his or her former sinful life ("wallowing in the mire" of sin or returning to vomit).

Other verses give warnings for Christians to "take heed" and "beware" such as I Corinthians 10:12: "Wherefore let him

that thinketh he standeth **TAKE HEED LEST HE FALL.**"
Peter cautions us: "Ye therefore, beloved, seeing ye know these
things before, **BEWARE LEST YE ALSO,** being led away
with the error of the wicked, **FALL FROM YOUR OWN
STEDFASTNESS**" (II Peter 3:17). In the Greek, the word
"fall" means to be driven out of one's course. Also, Hebrews
4:11 states: "Let us labour therefore to enter into that rest, **LEST
ANY MAN FALL** after the same example of unbelief."

FIVE "I WILLS"

Now, let's look at some very specific examples of backsliding. Let's start with Lucifer. In Ezekiel 28:15 we find: "Thou
wast **perfect** in thy ways from the day that thou wast created,
till iniquity was found in thee." John 8:44 states that He
"ABODE NOT in the truth." He had the truth but at some
point he turned from obeying it. His iniquity is found in Isaiah
14:12-15:

> How art thou fallen from heaven, O Lucifer, son
> of the morning! how art thou cut down to the ground,
> which didst weaken the nations! For thou hast said in
> thine heart, **I will** ascend into heaven, **I will** exalt my
> throne above the stars of God: **I will** sit also upon the
> mount of the congregation, in the sides of the north: **I
> will** ascend above the heights of the clouds; **I will** be
> like the most High. Yet thou shalt be brought down to
> hell, to the sides of the pit.

Jesus also said: "I beheld Satan as lightning fall from
heaven" (Luke 10:18).

It's true that Lucifer (now Satan) was not saved in the
same sense that Christians are saved today but he was a son of
God (Job 1:6; 2:1) and **PERFECT UNTIL** iniquity was found
and then he was cast forth as an **abominable branch** (Isaiah

14:19; Compare to John 15). Just because he "professed" that he would go to the highest position did not bring it to pass for **INIQUITY** was found and he was cast out. Now, if "once a son, always a son" is true, then Satan is still a son of God. What blasphemy!

The next example is of the angels who were also created perfect, yet 1/3 of the angels fell with Satan when he was cast out of heaven (Revelation 12:4). Revelation 12:7-9 explains:

> There was war in heaven: Michael and his angels fought against the dragon; and the dragon fought and his angels, And prevailed not; neither was their place found any more in heaven. And the great dragon was cast out, that old serpent, called the Devil, and Satan, which deceiveth the whole world: he was cast out into the earth, and his angels were cast out with him.

II Peter 2:4 states: **"God spared not the angels that sinned, but cast them down to hell,** and delivered them into chains of darkness, to be reserved unto judgment." Also, Jude 1:6: "The angels which **kept not their first estate,** but left their own habitation, He hath reserved in everlasting chains under darkness unto the judgment of the great day."

Those who sin will join Satan and the angels in their fate. Matthew 25:31-33, 41 reveals:

> When the Son of man shall come in His glory, and all the holy angels with Him, then shall He sit upon the throne of His glory: And before Him shall be gathered all nations: and He shall separate them one from another, as a shepherd divideth his sheep from the goats: And He shall set the sheep on his right hand, but the goats on the left....Then shall He say also unto them on the left hand, Depart from Me, ye cursed, into everlasting fire, prepared for the devil and his angels.

Adam (a son of God—Luke 3:38) and Eve also were created perfect, but they forfeited their eternal life by sin. God told Adam: "Of the tree of the knowledge of good and evil, thou shalt not eat of it: for **in the day** that thou eatest thereof **thou shalt surely die**" (Genesis 2:17). We know that Adam and Eve died **spiritually** the day they disobeyed. God cannot lie and since Adam did not die physically the day he ate of the fruit of the tree, we know the death being referred to is a **spiritual** death. Paul says: "Wherefore, as by one man sin entered into the world, and death by sin; and so death passed upon all men, for that all have sinned" (Romans 5:12).

Adam was put out of the Garden of Eden so that he would not be able to partake of the tree of life. This is the same tree we find mentioned in Revelation. Here we find those who are allowed to taste of this tree: "Blessed are they that **do His commandments,** that they may have right to the tree of life, and may enter in through the gates into the city" (Revelation 22:14). Who has the right to this tree? Only those who **DO HIS COMMANDMENTS.**

GOD IS DEPARTED

Let's now look at King Saul. At one time King Saul was a good man and saved for we find in I Samuel 10:10 that "the spirit of God came upon him" and verse 9 says that **"God gave him another heart."** However, I Samuel 16:14 SHOWS THAT SAUL BACKSLID: "The spirit of the Lord **departed** from Saul, and an evil spirit from the Lord troubled him." Also, I Samuel 18:12: "Saul was afraid of David, because **the Lord** was with him, and **was departed from Saul."**

God also told Samuel: "It repenteth Me that I have set up Saul to be king: for he is **TURNED BACK** from following Me, and hath not performed My commandments." The background to this verse reveals that God commanded the Israelites to destroy all the cattle and people of Amalek. Saul, nonetheless, spared King Agag and the best of the cattle. Saul then **LIED** to Samuel by saying: "I have performed the commandments of the Lord" (I Samuel 15:13). Samuel asked why he heard sheep bleating if Saul had obeyed God. Saul was quick to respond that the best of the oxen and sheep were saved so that they could sacrifice to God.

Samuel told Saul that God had talked to him and asked why he did not obey. **AGAIN, SAUL LIED**: "Yea, I have obeyed the voice of the Lord" (I Samuel 15:20). Samuel proceeds to answer: "Behold, to obey is better than sacrifice, and to hearken than the fat of rams. **FOR REBELLION IS AS THE SIN OF WITCHCRAFT, AND STUBBORN-NESS IS AS INIQUITY AND IDOLATRY.** Because thou hast rejected the word of the Lord, He hath also rejected thee from being king" (I Samuel 15:22b-23).

When Saul heard that the Lord had rejected him from being king he confessed: "**I HAVE SINNED:** for I have trans-gressed the commandment of the Lord, and thy words: because **I FEARED THE PEOPLE,** and obeyed their voice. Now therefore, I pray thee, pardon my sin, and turn again with me, that I may worship the Lord" (I Samuel 15:24-25). Samuel reiterated that the Lord had rejected Saul from being king and said that he would not return with Saul. As Samuel departed, Saul laid hold on his garment and it tore. Samuel said that Saul's kingdom would be torn away from him just as Samuel's garment had been rent. Once again Saul says: "**I HAVE SINNED:** yet honour me now, I pray thee, before the elders of my people and before Israel" (I Samuel 15:30).

Yes, after Saul was caught, he confessed that he had sinned but it is obvious by reading this setting that Saul only confessed in hopes of regaining his kingdom and having the people look up to him and honour him. This same thing is happening in the church today. People will lose their own soul trying to please and gain other people's praise and favor rather than obeying God's Word.

Saul, who was one time saved, had so backslidden that he eventually visited a witch. Remember, Galatians 5:19-21 tells us that witchcraft is one of the sins of the flesh and no one who does any such thing can enter heaven.

When the Lord would no longer answer Saul, he turned to a witch to try to contact Samuel for him. Saul admitted to Samuel: **"God is departed from me, and answereth me no more,** neither by prophets, nor by dreams: therefore I have called thee, that thou mayest make known unto me what I shall do" (I Samuel 28:15). Samuel said to Saul: "Wherefore then dost thou ask of me, seeing the **LORD IS DEPARTED FROM THEE, AND IS BECOME THINE ENEMY?"** (I Samuel 28:16).

I Chronicles 10:13 declares: "So Saul died for his **transgression** which he committed against the Lord, even against the word of the Lord, which he kept not, and also for asking counsel of one that had a familiar spirit, to inquire of it." He finally ended up committing suicide (I Samuel 31:4; I Chronicles 10:4). As you know, suicide is self-murder and I John 3:15 says: "Ye know that <u>no</u> murderer hath eternal life abiding in him."

NEEDED: TRUE REPENTANCE

Confession alone was not enough to save Saul and it will not be enough to save you unless there is **TRUE REPENT-ANCE.** "He that covereth his sins shall not prosper: but whoso **confesseth and forsaketh** them shall have mercy" (Proverbs 28:13).

Demas is another case of a backslider. He was one of Paul's fellow laborers (Philemon 1:24; Colossians 4:14), however Paul said: "Demas hath forsaken me, having loved this present world" (II Timothy 4:10). I John 2:15 warns us: "Love not the world, neither the things that are in the world. **If any man love the world, the love of the Father is not in him.**"

Alexander and Hymenaeus are two more examples. In Paul's admonition to Timothy, we find: **"Holding faith,** and a good conscience; which some **having put away concerning faith have made shipwreck:** Of whom is Hymenaeus and Alexander; whom I have delivered unto Satan, that they may learn not to blaspheme" (I Timothy 1:19). Hymenaeus is mentioned again in II Timothy 2:17: "Their word will eat as doth a canker: of whom is Hymenaeus and Philetus; **Who concerning the truth have erred,** saying that the resurrection is past already; and overthrow the faith of some."

Covetousness caused some people to backslide for I Timothy 6:10 says: "For the love of money is the root of all evil: which while some coveted after, **they have erred from the faith,** and pierced themselves through with many sorrows."

ANOTHER BACKSLIDER

Simon coveted power and he backslid. Look at Acts 8:13-24:

Then Simon himself believed also: and when he was baptized, he continued with Philip, and wondered, beholding the miracles and signs which were done. Now when the apostles which were at Jerusalem heard that Samaria had received the word of God, they sent unto them Peter and John: Who, when they were come down, prayed for them, that they might receive the Holy Ghost: (For as yet he was fallen upon none of them: only they were baptized in the name of the Lord Jesus.) Then laid they their hands on them, and they received the Holy Ghost. And when Simon saw that through laying on of the apostles' hands the Holy Ghost was given, he offered them money, Saying, Give me also this power, that on whomsoever I lay hands, he may receive the Holy Ghost. But Peter said unto him, Thy money perish with thee, because thou hast thought that the gift of God may be purchased with money. Thou hast neither part nor lot in this matter: for thy heart is not right in the sight of God. Repent therefore of this thy wickedness, and pray God, if perhaps the thought of thine heart may be forgiven thee. For I perceive that thou art in the gall of bitterness, and in the bond of iniquity. Then answered Simon, and said, Pray ye to the Lord for me, that none of these things which ye have spoken come upon me.

Again, many claim that Simon was never saved to begin with, but the Bible clearly refutes this. It states: **"Simon himself BELIEVED also."** Can it be **ANY** clearer? After he believed, he was baptized and continued on with Philip. When he saw the miracles that they were doing, he offered to pay them in order to receive this same kind of power. Peter then rebuked him and said **"thy heart is not right** in the sight of God. **Repent** therefore of this thy **wickedness."** He added that he perceived that he was in the "gall of bitterness."

Now Ephesians 4:31 tells the Christian: "Let all **bitterness,** and wrath, and anger, and clamour, and evil speaking, be put away from you, with all malice: And be ye kind one to another, tenderhearted, forgiving one another, even as God for Christ's sake hath forgiven you. Be ye therefore followers of God, as dear children." Even stronger is Hebrews 12:15: "Looking **diligently** lest any man fail of the grace of God; lest any root of **bitterness** springing up trouble you, and **thereby many be defiled."**

Thankfully, Simon immediately recognized his wrong and said: "Pray ye to the Lord for me, that none of these things which ye have spoken come upon me." He didn't call Peter a liar and say that he was eternally secure and didn't have to repent. He was not rebellious but humble and asked for forgiveness.

LET'S NOT RUN IN VAIN

Paul certainly recognized that people could be saved and then backslide. In referring to the Galatians, he said: "My little children, of whom I **travail in birth again** until Christ be formed in you" (Galatians 4:19). Paul also realized that his labor could be **in vain** if he didn't hold to the Word of God: "Holding forth the word of life; that I may rejoice in the day of Christ, that I have not run **in vain,** neither laboured **in vain**" (Philippians 2:16). He also worried that many of his efforts would be in vain if people didn't hold firm: "I am afraid of you, lest I have bestowed upon you labour **in vain**" (Galatians 4:11). "For this cause, when I could no longer forbear, I sent to know your faith, **lest** by some means the tempter have tempted you, and **our labour be in vain**" (I Thessalonians 3:5). "We then, as workers together with Him, beseech you also that ye **receive not the grace of God in vain**" (II Corinthians 6:1).

In John 6:66 we find that many people forsook Christ: "From that time many of **His disciples** went back, and **walked no more** with Him." When this happened, Jesus asked the twelve: "Will ye also go away?" (John 6:67). "Then Simon Peter answered Him, Lord, to whom shall we go? Thou hast the words of eternal life" (John 6:68). Yet, Peter himself had his moment of backsliding. Jesus had forewarned Peter that he would deny Christ, but Peter (as well as all of the other disciples) said that he never would do such a thing (Matthew 26:34-35; Mark 14:30-31; Luke 22:34). Jesus said to him:

Simon, Simon, behold, Satan hath desired to have you, that he may sift you as wheat: But I have prayed for thee, that thy faith fail not: and **WHEN THOU ART CONVERTED**, strengthen thy brethren" (Luke 22:31-32).

In spite of Peter's insistence that he would never deny Christ, when Jesus was arrested and being mocked, Peter was **fearful** to be known as one of Christ's disciples and he did deny Jesus. Jesus foreknew that this would happen and that is why He warned Peter.

In Revelation 21:8 we discover that: "The **fearful**, and unbelieving, and the abominable, and murderers, and whore-mongers, and sorcerers, and idolaters, and all liars, shall have their part in the lake which burneth with fire and brimstone: which is the second death." The word "fearful" comes from a Greek word referring to those who had retreated and renounced Christ in the face of persecution. Revelation 2:10 says: "Fear none of those things which thou shalt suffer: behold, the devil shall cast some of you into prison, that ye may be tried; and ye shall have tribulation ten days: **BE THOU FAITHFUL UNTO DEATH, AND I WILL GIVE THEE A CROWN OF LIFE.**" To receive the crown of life, one must be faithful unto death—even if we are persecuted for Christ's sake. If we retreat out of fear, we will lose our eternal life. In Peter's case, he backslid because of fear of persecution.

Notice also II Timothy 2:12 **"IF WE SUFFER, WE SHALL ALSO REIGN WITH HIM: IF WE DENY HIM, HE ALSO WILL DENY US"** and Matthew 10:33: **"WHO-SOEVER SHALL DENY ME BEFORE MEN, HIM WILL I ALSO DENY BEFORE MY FATHER WHICH IS IN HEAVEN."**

Peter, however, realized the sin he committed and he "wept bitterly" (Matthew 26:75; Mark 14:72; Luke 22:62) and repented.

After this Peter was very bold under persecution and history tells us that he was martyred for Christ's sake. When it came time to face death, Peter who was to be crucified, felt so unworthy to die in the same manner as Christ did, that he requested to be put upside down on the cross. Yes, some backsliders can and do repent, but unless they repent, they will not be saved.

CAST ME NOT AWAY

Proverbs 14:14 tells us: "The backslider in heart shall be filled with his own ways" but, thank God, <u>backsliders can be restored</u>. In Jeremiah 3:22 God says: **"Return, ye backsliding children, and I will heal your backslidings."** Also, Jeremiah 3:12-13:

Return, thou backsliding Israel, saith the Lord; and I will not cause Mine anger to fall upon you: for I am merciful, saith the Lord, and I will not keep anger for ever. ONLY ACKNOWLEDGE THINE INIQUITY, that thou has transgressed against the Lord thy God...and ye have not obeyed My voice, saith the Lord.

Let's look at one more example of a backslider in this chapter. King David was a man after God's own heart (I Samuel 13:14; Acts 13:22), yet he sinned on two occasions. One time David decided to number Israel and even though his captains tried to prevent him from doing so, David's command prevailed. So Israel was numbered (it took about 10 months—II Samuel 24:8) and the total was given to David. "And David's heart smote him after that he had numbered the people. And David said unto the Lord, I HAVE SINNED greatly in that I have done..." (II Samuel 24:10a). David confessed his sin but he did not stop there, but continued with his prayer: "Now, I beseech Thee, O Lord, take away the iniquity of Thy servant; for I have done very foolishly" (II Samuel 24:10b). David's sin cost the lives of 70,000 men (II Samuel 24:15).

On one other occasion David sinned and that was when he committed adultery with Bathsheba. David even went so far as to have her husband put to death and this greatly displeased the Lord, so the Lord sent Nathan, the prophet, to David. Nathan used a parable about a rich man and a poor man. David became angry at the rich man who had many sheep and yet took a poor man's only lamb. Nathan then said to David: "Thou art the man" (II Samuel 12:7). He also said that "the sword shall never depart from thine house" (II Samuel 12:10). David confessed: "**I HAVE SINNED** against the Lord. And Nathan said unto David, The Lord also **hath put away thy sin; thou shalt not die.** Howbeit, because by this deed thou hast given great occasion to the enemies of the Lord to blaspheme, the child also that is born unto thee shall surely die" (II Samuel 12:13-14).

It is wonderful that David confessed his sin and that he also forsook it, but the consequences of his sin were not limited to him. Many innocent people of his household had to pay for David's sin and he also gave his enemies an occasion to blaspheme. Again, we see that the family and other innocent people suffered because of one's sin. Also, David lost a son. How many people have lost their children (physically and spiritually) before they return to the Lord? We must remember that if we should sin that many other innocent people may also be hurt and lost because of our sin.

David was caught and that probably prompted his confession of "**I HAVE SINNED**," but David did **truly repent** for we are told that Psalm 51 was written when Nathan came to him to tell him of his sin with Bathsheba. In this Psalm David prays:

Have mercy upon me, O God...blot out my transgressions. Wash me throughly from mine iniquity, and cleanse me from my sin. For I acknowledge my transgressions: and my sin is ever before me. Against Thee, Thee only, have I sinned, and done this evil in Thy sight....Purge me with hyssop, and I shall be clean: wash me, and I shall be whiter than snow. Make me to hear joy and gladness; that the bones which Thou hast broken may rejoice. Hide Thy face from my sins, and blot out all mine iniquities. **Create** in me a clean heart, O God; and **renew** a right spirit within me. **Cast me not away from Thy presence;** and **take not Thy holy spirit from me.** Restore unto me the joy of Thy salvation; and uphold me with Thy free spirit. (Psalm 51:1-12, in part)

We can see that David not only made a confession but that he truly repented of his sin. There are several things that take place when sin is confessed and repented of.

TRUE REPENTANCE

* They are blotted out—"I have blotted out, as a thick cloud, thy transgressions, and, as a cloud, thy sins: return unto Me; for I have redeemed thee" (Isaiah 44:22).

* They are forgiven—"If we confess our sins, He is faithful and just to forgive us our sins, and to cleanse us from all unrighteousness" (I John 1:9).

* They are forgotten—"For I will be merciful to their unrighteousness, and their sins and their iniquities will I remember no more" (Hebrews 8:12).

* They are covered—"Blessed is he whose transgression is forgiven, whose sin is covered [by the blood]" (Psalm 32:1).

* They are washed away—"Unto him that loved us, and washed us from our sins in His own blood" (Revelation 1:5).

* They are taken away—"And ye know that He was manifested to take away our sins; and in Him is no sin" (I John 3:5).

* One is saved from them—"And she shall bring forth a son, and thou shalt call His name Jesus: for He shall save His people from their sins" (Matthew 1:21).

* One is cleansed from them—"But if we walk in the light, as He is in the light, we have fellowship one with another, and the blood of Jesus Christ His Son cleanseth us from all sin" (I John 1:7).

* One becomes dead to them—"Who His own self bare our sins in His own body on the tree, that we, being dead to sins, should live unto righteousness: by Whose stripes ye were healed" (I Peter 2:24).

AM I BECOME YOUR ENEMY?

Today we see so many in the church who will confess "**I HAVE SINNED**" when they are caught, but these people continue on in their sin and never fully repent and **forsake** their sin, but there is forgiveness waiting for us if we sincerely want to go with God. Saul confessed to Samuel that he had sinned but his confession **DID NOT** stop him from trying to kill David on numerous occasions. He even tried to kill his own son, Jonathan (I Samuel 20:32-33). Saul threw javelins at David and Jonathan because they were righteous. Cain killed his brother because Abel was righteous (I John 3:12). Queen Jezebel had Naboth killed because he obeyed God instead of man (I Kings 21:1-20). The princes cast Jeremiah into the prison because he prophesied evil against them. They could not accept the truth from a righteous man (Jeremiah 38:1-6). Paul asked the Galatians:

"Am I therefore become your enemy, because I tell you the truth?" (Galatians 4:16).

Isn't it the same today in spiritual terms? Some will hate me for telling the truth about the "false security," but you are only harming yourselves—not me. It's **YOUR** eternal welfare that is at stake. Of course, how many people are being sent to hell because you tell them that they are still saved even though they are sinning? Are your children and loved ones going to go to hell because of you twisting the Scriptures? Are your neighbors being led in a false way because of your lifestyle?

The Sauls of today still throw their javelins of gossip and lies about the men of God. Cain still rises up and kills his brother's reputation because of jealousy. The Jezebels kill the righteous men's characters by spreading lies around. The princes (the leaders of their day) still bind the Jeremiahs of our day when they have the spiritual backbone to preach the truth even though it pierces some hearts. There are some in the church who will confess that they have done wrong, but they will **CONTINUE** to do the same thing as before their confession. Then, because some of these people have been caught in their sin they decide that they need a different pastor or a different church. Some people will even move to a new area, but **NONE** of these things will clear or cleanse the heart.

We need to do our first works over (Revelation 2:5) and to make our wrongs right. We will not receive God's favor by just confessing or by blaming someone else for our failure. We **OURSELVES** must **FULLY REPENT**, make our wrongs right to the best of our ability, and then **FORSAKE** that sin.

DON'T JUST COVER THE RUST

One story I read illustrates the point quite well. One man had repeatedly painted his rusty patio furniture but what he really needed to do was to sand off the rust first and then paint it. He finally decided that he would take care of this problem so he stripped off all the paint that had accumulated and then took a rust remover to the rust that had been bleeding through the paint. All he had been doing before was covering up the rust instead of **REMOVING** it, but rust, like sin, continues to eat through whatever is covering it up.

In order to get rid of the problem of sin, we must not only confess our sin (cover up the rust), we must actually get to the root of the problem and have the sin **REMOVED** if we wish to continue on in our Christian walk unhindered. Many people try to cover the external part, but they fail to take care of the real or internal problem. For us to have a victorious walk with Christ and to be secure in Christ, we must make sure that we do not only "confess" that we have sinned, but we must actually truly repent of our sins, and then **FORSAKE** them.

Here are some secrets of how to have victory over sin found in Psalm 119. They are:

✞ Taking heed to God's Word—"Wherewithal shall a young man cleanse his way? by taking heed thereto according to Thy word" (v.9).

✞ Seeking God whole-heartedly—"With my whole heart have I sought Thee: O let me not wander from Thy commandments" (v.10).

✞ Hiding God's Word in one's heart—"Thy word have I hid in mine heart, that **I might not sin against Thee**" (v.11).

✞ Removing lying from one's way—"Remove from me the way of lying" (v.29).

✞ Delighting in God's Word—"Thy law is my delight" (v.77).

✟ Meditating on God's Word—"Thy testimonies are my meditation" (v.99).

✟ Refraining from every evil way—"I have refrained my feet from every evil way, that I might keep Thy word" (v.101).

✟ Hating every false way—"I hate every false way" (v.104).

✟ Determining to obey to the end—**"I have inclined mine heart to perform Thy statutes alway, <u>even unto the end</u>"** (v.112).

Following these guidelines, we will be **secure in Christ.** "Keep yourselves in the love of God, looking for the mercy of our Lord Jesus Christ unto eternal life" (Jude 1:21).

Chapter Eight

WAS JUDAS EVER SAVED?

There is much controversy concerning Judas. Some people contend that he was never saved. Others insist that he was saved. Even though he betrayed Jesus and committed suicide, some teach that he still went to heaven. Once again, we need to return to the Bible to see what it clearly teaches us about this issue.

If we search the Scriptures, it is clear to see that Judas, like Saul, was at one time saved, but that he, too, was a backslider. Here was a man who saw the many miracles of Jesus. He saw the blind receive their sight, he witnessed the demons being cast out, he looked on as the deaf were healed and he saw the dead rise again. In fact, he even had done many miracles himself. Turn to Matthew 10:1-8:

> And when He had called unto Him His twelve disciples, He gave them power against unclean spirits, to cast them out, and to heal all manner of sickness and all manner of disease. Now the names of the twelve apostles are these; The first, Simon, who is called Peter, and Andrew his brother; James the son of Zebedee, and John his brother; Philip, and Bartholomew; Thomas, and Matthew the publican; James the son of Alphaeus, and Lebbaeus, whose surname was Thaddaeus; Simon the Canaanite, and **Judas Iscariot, who also betrayed**

Him. These twelve **Jesus sent forth,** and commanded them, saying, Go not into the way of the Gentiles, and into any city of the Samaritans enter ye not: But go rather to the lost sheep of the house of Israel. And as ye go, **preach,** saying, The kingdom of heaven is at hand. **Heal the sick, cleanse the lepers, raise the dead, cast out devils: freely ye have received, freely give.** (See also Mark 3:14-15; 6:7; and Luke 9:1-2.)

Mark 6:12-13 tells us: "And they went out, and preached that men should repent. And they cast out many devils, and anointed with oil many that were sick, and healed them." Judas, as well as the other 11 apostles, healed the sick and cast out demons. In Luke 10:17-20 we find that Jesus sent out seventy disciples to do the same thing.

And the seventy returned again with joy, saying, Lord, even the devils are subject unto us through Thy name. And He said unto them,...Behold, I give unto you power to tread on serpents and scorpions, and over all the power of the enemy: and nothing shall by any means hurt you. Notwithstanding in this rejoice not, that the spirits are subject unto you; but rather rejoice, **because your names are written in heaven.**

SHEEP AMONG WOLVES

Yes, Judas was a saved person. In fact, in Psalms 41:9 is a prophecy concerning Jesus' betrayal by Judas: "Yea, mine **own familiar friend, in whom I trusted,** which did eat of My bread, hath lifted up his heel against Me." Notice that Jesus trusted Judas and considered him to be His "familiar friend." Would He trust a sinner like this?

In Matthew 10:16 we see that Jesus sent the twelve (Judas included) "as sheep in the midst of wolves." Judas was not considered to be a wolf—he was called a sheep. In this same passage we see that Jesus is forewarning the disciples that they will be persecuted for **HIS** sake. He then adds: "But when they deliver you up, take no thought how or what ye shall speak: for it shall be given you in that same hour what ye shall speak. For it is not ye that speak, but the **Spirit of your Father which speaketh in you**" (Matthew 10:19-20). Do you see that the Spirit of God was **IN** Judas?

We also discover that Judas was evidently a Bishop of a church for in Acts we see that it was prophesied that someone else should take his bishoprick (Acts 1:20). Now the Bible gives some very specific instructions for a bishop:

> This is a true saying, If a man desire the office of a bishop, he desireth a good work. A bishop then must be blameless, the husband of one wife, vigilant, sober, of good behaviour, given to hospitality, apt to teach; Not given to wine, no striker, not greedy of filthy lucre; but patient, not a brawler, not covetous; One that ruleth well his own house, having his children in subjection with all gravity; (For if a man know not how to rule his own house, how shall he take care of the church of God?)...Moreover he must have a good report of them which are without; lest he fall into reproach and the snare of the devil. (I Timothy 3:1-5, 7)

> For a bishop must be blameless, as the steward of God; not selfwilled, not soon angry, not given to wine, no striker, not given to filthy lucre; But a lover of hospitality, a lover of good men, sober, just, holy, temperate; **Holding fast the faithful word** as he hath been taught, that he may be able by sound doctrine both to exhort and to convince the gainsayers. (Titus 1:7-9)

Obviously, a bishop must be a saved person—and he must live a righteous and holy life according to the Bible. Would

Jesus have chosen a sinner to hold such an office in contradiction to these qualifications? Of course not!

SATAN ENTERED IN

Somewhere along the line, however, Judas' heart became hardened and eventually he went so far as to betray his Master for 30 pieces of silver—only the price of a slave. In John 13:27 we see that it was after communion that Satan actually entered Judas: "And after the sop **Satan** <u>entered</u> **into him."** (See also Luke 22:3.) There are two things that need to be noticed here. First is that Satan had to have been out of Judas to enter into him. Second is that once a person relinquishes control to Satan, he is no longer a child of God. "No man can serve two masters: for either he will hate the one, and love the other; or else he will hold to the one, and despise the other. **Ye cannot serve God and mammon**" (Matthew 6:24; Luke 16:13). "Know ye not, that **to whom ye yield yourselves servants to obey, his servants ye are to whom ye obey;** whether of sin unto death, or of obedience unto righteousness?" (Romans 6:16). "Whosoever committeth sin is the servant of sin" (John 8:34b).

However, there is even stronger evidence than this that Judas was saved and then backslid and went to hell. Turn to Acts 1:16-18, 20, 25:

> Men and brethren, this scripture must needs have been fulfilled, which the Holy Ghost by the mouth of David spake before concerning Judas, which was guide to them that took Jesus. For **he was numbered with us, and had obtained part of this ministry.** Now this man purchased a field with the reward of iniquity; and falling headlong, he burst asunder in the midst, and all his bowels gushed out....For it is <u>written in the book of Psalms,</u> Let his habitation be desolate, and let no man dwell therein: and his bishoprick let another

take....That he may take part of this ministry and apostleship, from which **Judas by transgression fell,** that he might go to his own place.

MESSIANIC PROPHECY

Since this is a prophecy from the book of Psalms, we also need to look at that passage. It is found in Psalm 69 and it is quite obvious that this is a Messianic prophecy:

They gave Me also gall for My meat; and in My thirst they gave Me vinegar to drink. Let their table become a snare before them: and that which should have been for their welfare, let it become a trap. Let their eyes be darkened, that they see not; and make their loins continually to shake. Pour out Thine indignation upon them, and let Thy wrathful anger take hold of them. **Let their habitation be desolate;** and let none dwell in their tents. For they persecute Him whom Thou hast smitten; and they talk to the grief of those whom Thou hast wounded. **Add iniquity unto their iniquity: and let them not come into Thy righteousness. Let them be blotted out of the book of the living, and not be written with the righteous.** (Psalm 69:21-28)

Do you see what this Scripture says? It says: **"LET THEM BE BLOTTED OUT OF THE BOOK OF THE LIV- ING"!** This is proof beyond a shadow of a doubt that Judas was saved and his name was blotted out. Jesus Himself said: "While I was with them in the world, I kept them in Thy name: those that Thou gavest Me I have kept, and **none of them is lost, but the son of perdition;** that the scripture might be fulfilled" (John 17:12).

After Judas betrayed Jesus, he had great remorse and confessed: **"I HAVE SINNED** in that I have betrayed innocent blood" (Matthew 27:4). Yes, Judas confessed but he went out and hung himself. Again, we see **CONFESSION** but **NO REAL REPENTANCE** and this resulted in Judas losing his salvation and going to hell. Jesus said: "No man, having put his hand to the plough, and looking back, is fit for the kingdom of God" (Luke 9:62). "Now the just shall live by faith: but if any man **DRAW BACK,** My soul shall have no pleasure in him" (Hebrews 10:38).

Chapter Nine

I WILL NEVER LEAVE THEE

"Let your conversation be without covetousness; and be content with such things as ye have: for <u>He hath said,</u> **I will never leave thee, nor forsake thee**" (Hebrews 13:5).

Does this verse mean that the Lord will never leave us even if we are living in sin? To find the answer to that, we need to turn to Joshua for that is where this reference is taken from.

There shall not any man be able to stand before thee all the days of thy life: as I was with Moses, so I will be with thee: **I will not fail thee, nor forsake thee.** Be strong and of a good courage: for unto this people shalt thou divide for an inheritance the land, which I sware unto their fathers to give them. **Only** be thou strong and very courageous, **that thou mayest observe to do according to <u>all</u> the law,** which Moses My servant commanded thee: **turn not from it to the right hand or to the left,** that thou mayest prosper whithersoever thou goest. This **book of the law shall not depart out of thy mouth;** but thou shalt meditate therein day and night, that thou mayest observe to **do according to all that is written therein:** for <u>then</u> thou shalt make thy way prosperous, and <u>then</u> thou shalt have good success. (Joshua 1:5-8)

It is clear to see that there were **conditions** attached to this promise. The Lord would not fail nor leave Joshua, but

Joshua was also commanded to obey God's Word. Then, and only then, would his way be prosperous and successful. The same is true for us today. Again, I repeat, we do have security in Christ—but it is based on our obedience to Him. "The Lord is with you, **while ye be with Him; and if ye seek Him, He will be found of you; but** *if ye forsake Him, He will forsake you"* (II Chronicles 15:2). The Bible message cannot be any clearer.

What is interesting is that shortly after the Lord promised Joshua that He would never leave him, He turned around and said that He would leave him. Is this a contradiction? Did God lie? Of course not. You see, there was "sin in the camp" and God **CANNOT** look on sin. Turn to Joshua 7. In this chapter we find that Joshua went to battle and Israel was defeated. When Joshua asked the Lord what was wrong, this was God's reply:

> Israel hath sinned, and they have also transgressed my covenant which I commanded them: for they have even taken of the accursed thing, and have also stolen, and dissembled also, and they have put it even among their own stuff. Therefore the children of Israel could not stand before their enemies, but turned their backs before their enemies, because they were accursed: **neither will I be with you any more, except ye destroy the accursed from among you.** (Joshua 7:11-12)

GOD KEEPS HIS PROMISES

God **ALWAYS** keeps His promise and He promised that if we sin, we cannot continue to be in communion with Him. Joshua 24:20 states: **"If ye forsake the Lord,** and serve strange gods, then **He will turn and do you hurt, and consume you, after** that **He hath done you good."**

Ezra said: "The hand of our God is upon all them for good that seek Him; but His power and His wrath is **against all them that forsake Him"** (Ezra 8:22). Obviously, the only ones who can forsake God are those who have already known Him. Sinners cannot forsake God. I cannot forsake my husband if I am not married. I cannot forsake adultery, if I've never committed it and I cannot forsake God if I've never known Him.

Below are just a few of the many verses along this line.

→ "He that turneth away his ear from hearing the law, even his prayer shall be abomination" (Proverbs 28:9).

→ "If I regard iniquity in my heart, the Lord will not hear me" (Psalm 66:18).

→ "As for such as turn aside unto their crooked ways, the Lord shall lead them forth with the workers of iniquity: but peace shall be upon Israel" (Psalm 125:5).

→ "He that saith, I know Him, and keepeth not His commandments, is a liar, and the truth is not in him" (I John 2:4).

→ "The Lord preserveth all them that love Him: but all the wicked will He destroy" (Psalm 145:20).

→ "Whoso walketh uprightly shall be saved: but he that is perverse in his ways shall fall at once" (Proverbs 28:18).

→ "Wherefore come out from among them, and be ye separate, saith the Lord, and touch not the unclean thing; and I will receive you" (II Corinthians 6:17).

→ "If ye keep My commandments, ye shall abide in My love; even as I have kept My Father's commandments, and abide in His love" (John 15:10).

→ "The destruction of the transgressors and of the sinners shall be together, and they that forsake the Lord shall be

<u>consumed</u>" (Isaiah 1:28). Notice that there are two separate categories here: the sinners <u>AND</u> those who forsake the Lord!

➔ "I will hear what God the Lord will speak: for He will speak peace unto His people, and to His saints: but **let them not turn again to folly**" (Psalms 85:8).

➔ "And Jesus said unto him, No man, having put his hand to the plough, and looking back, is fit for the kingdom of God" (Luke 9:62).

➔ "If thou wilt return, O Israel, saith the Lord, return unto Me: and **if thou wilt put away thine abominations** out of My sight, **then shalt thou not remove**" (Jeremiah 4:1).

➔ "Israel, <u>return</u> unto the Lord thy God; for <u>thou hast fallen by thine iniquity</u>" (Hosea 14:1).

➔ "And them that are <u>turned back from the Lord</u>; and <u>those that have not sought the Lord</u>, nor inquired for Him" (Zephaniah 1:6). Again notice the two separate categories: those who have turned back and those who have never sought the Lord.

➔ "But <u>they rebelled</u>, and vexed His holy Spirit: therefore <u>He was turned</u> to be their enemy, and <u>He fought against them</u>" (Isaiah 63:10).

➔ "He also shall be my salvation: for an hypocrite shall not come before Him" (Job 13:16).

➔ "For what is the hope of the hypocrite, though he hath gained, when **God taketh away his soul?**" (Job 27:8).

➔ "If any man defile the temple of God, **him shall God destroy;** for the temple of God is holy, which temple ye are" (I Corinthians 3:17). This is obviously referring to the Christian for it says we are God's temple ("which temple ye are") but if **ANY MAN** defile this temple, **"him shall God DESTROY."**

↝ "Even from the days of your fathers ye are gone away from Mine ordinances, and have not kept them. **Return unto Me, and I will return unto you,** saith the Lord of hosts. But ye said, Wherein shall we return?" (Malachi 3:7).

↝ "<u>Ye are</u> the salt of the earth: <u>but if</u> the salt have lost his savour, wherewith shall it be salted? **it is thenceforth good for nothing, but to be cast out,** and to be trodden under foot of men" (Matthew 5:13).

↝ "Ye therefore, beloved, seeing ye know these things before, <u>beware lest ye also,</u> **being led away with the error of the wicked,** <u>fall from your own stedfastness</u>" (II Peter 3:17).

↝ "Remember therefore from whence <u>thou art fallen,</u> and <u>repent,</u> and <u>do the first works;</u> <u>or else</u> I will come unto thee quickly, and will remove thy candlestick out of his place, <u>except thou repent</u>" (Revelation 2:5).

↝ "Whosoever transgresseth, and **ABIDETH NOT IN THE DOCTRINE OF CHRIST,** <u>hath not God.</u> **He that abideth in the doctrine of Christ, he hath both the Father and the Son**" (II John 1:9). Remember, I **CANNOT** possibly abide (remain, stay, dwell) in some place that I've <u>never</u> been. I cannot remain in Australia if I've never been there and no one can remain in Christ unless he has been in Christ.

ALL SCRIPTURE IS PROFITABLE

Remember: **ALL** scripture is given by inspiration of God, and is profitable **for doctrine, for reproof, for correction, for instruction in righteousness**" (II Timothy 3:16).

These verses are explicit and no one should deny the clear teaching of Scripture. Why do we try to **CHANGE** the specific meaning to say something that isn't being taught? When we do so, we are only twisting the Scriptures unto our own damnation (see II Peter 3:16). We are hurting ourselves (and all those who are depending on us to teach the truth). Malachi 2:17 states: "Ye have wearied the Lord with your words. Yet ye say, Wherein have we wearied Him? When ye say, **Every one that doeth evil is good in the sight of the Lord, and He delighteth in them;** or, Where is the God of judgment?"

Also, the prophets of Ezekiel's day were promising **life** to the wicked. This is what is still being done today when many people promise those living in sin that they are still saved and have eternal life. Let us not be guilty as the false prophets were:

> "Because <u>with lies</u> ye have made the heart of the righteous sad, whom I have not made sad; and <u>strengthened the hands of the wicked</u>, **THAT HE SHOULD NOT RETURN FROM HIS WICKED WAY, <u>BY PROMISING HIM LIFE</u>"** (Ezekiel 13:22).

Chapter Ten

PAST, PRESENT, AND FUTURE SINS

Many radio and TV preachers today claim that **ALL** of our sins are forgiven—past, present, and future sins. They say this to try to "prove" that no matter what sins we commit after we come to Christ, they are all forgiven and taken care of. Is this Biblical doctrine?

"**If** we confess our sins, He is faithful and just to forgive us our sins, and to cleanse us from all unrighteousness" (I John 1:9). Once again, when we go to the Bible we see that there is a **CONDITION** attached. The condition of having our sins forgiven is that we **CONFESS** them. Since I can't know what sins I may commit in the future, I can't confess them, therefore my sins are not forgiven in advance. You will not find **ONE VERSE** that says that all past, present, and future sins are forgiven when we get saved. You will find, however, that **ONLY** our past sins are forgiven. Let's look at Romans 3:25: "Whom God hath set forth to be a propitiation through faith in His blood, to declare His righteousness for the **REMISSION OF SINS THAT ARE PAST,** through the forbearance of God." See also II Peter 1:9: "But he that lacketh these things is blind, and cannot see afar off, and hath forgotten that he was **PURGED FROM HIS OLD SINS.**" If ALL our future sins were covered prior to our confession of them, then there would be **NO NEED** of an Advocate, but we do have an Advocate according to I John 2:1.

Now let's suppose that I have a friend who promises to pay all my bills when I notify him of them. After I run up a big printing expense for my books, I go to him and ask him to pay my debt. He willingly does it. I then run up another large bill. After several months the printer contacts me and says that I have a debt that needs to be paid. I say that I don't have any debt because the debt was already **PAID IN FULL.** Do you think the printer would accept this explanation? Of course not. After the debt has been incurred, I need to go back to my friend and tell him that I accumulated another bill that needs to be met. Once I confess I have another bill to be paid, He will once again pay it in full—up to that point in time. My debt will be covered by my friend but I must admit that there is a debt that needs to be paid. The same is true with Christ. He has paid the price for our sins up to the point of our conversion but if we sin after that, the new sin must be confessed so that the blood of Christ can be applied to our heart again.

Remember: "But fornication, and all uncleanness, or covetousness, **let it not be <u>once</u> named among you,** as becometh saints" (Ephesians 5:3). We are not to sin, but IF we do sin, John says: "My little children, these things write I unto you, that ye **sin not.** And if any man sin, we have an advocate with the Father, Jesus Christ the righteous" (I John 2:1) and "If we confess our sins, He is faithful and just to forgive us our sins, and to cleanse us from all unrighteousness" (I John 1:9).

SEPARATED UNTO GOD

There is a principle in Scripture that pertains to this very thought. Although it is not speaking specifically of the salvation of the believer, we know that **ALL** Scripture is profitable for doctrine and instruction (II Timothy 3:16). The passage we need to look at is found in Numbers 6:2-12. When an Israelite made a vow to separate himself unto the Lord, there were certain qualifications that needed to be met. All during his time of separation he had to be holy and he was forbidden to come near a dead body. He was not allowed to "make himself unclean for his father, or for his mother, for his brother, or for his sister, when they die: because the consecration of his God is upon his head. All the days of his separation he is holy unto the Lord."

Now, what if something happened during this time and he became defiled? The Bible answers that question. It tells us that if someone suddenly died near him and he became defiled, then he would have to offer a sin offering and have an atonement made for him. In addition, all "the days that were before shall be lost, because his separation was defiled."

The same principle can be correlated to our Christian life. If we commit sin, we need to have Christ's sacrifice applied again—but all our previous righteous is not credited to our account. Turn to Ezekiel 18:24-32:

> When the **righteous turneth away** from his righteousness, and **committeth iniquity,** and doeth according to all the abominations that the wicked man doeth, shall he live? **All his righteousness that he hath done shall not be mentioned:** in his trespass that he hath trespassed, and in his sin that he hath sinned, in them shall he die. Yet ye say, The way of the Lord is not equal. Hear now, O house of Israel; Is not My way equal? are not your ways unequal? **When a righteous man turneth away from his righteousness, and committeth iniquity, and dieth in them; for his iniquity that he hath done shall he die.** Again, when the wicked man turneth away from his wickedness that he hath committed, and doeth that which is lawful and right, he shall save his soul alive. Because he considereth, and turneth away from all his transgressions that he hath committed, he shall surely live, he shall not die. Yet saith the house of Israel, The

way of the Lord is not equal. O house of Israel, are not My ways equal? are not your ways unequal? Therefore I will judge you, O house of Israel, every one according to his ways, saith the Lord God. **Repent, and turn yourselves from all your transgressions; so iniquity shall not be your ruin.** Cast away from you all your transgressions, whereby ye have transgressed; and make you a new heart and a new spirit: for why will ye die, O house of Israel? For I have no pleasure in the death of him that dieth, saith the Lord God: wherefore turn yourselves, and live ye. (See also Ezekiel 3:18-21.)

PREVIEOUS RIGHTEOUSNESS LOST

THE RIGHTEOUSNESS OF THE RIGHTEOUS SHALL NOT DELIVER HIM IN THE DAY OF HIS TRANSGRESSION: as for the wickedness of the wicked, he shall not fall thereby in the day that he turneth from his wickedness; **NEITHER SHALL THE RIGHTEOUS BE ABLE TO LIVE FOR HIS RIGHTEOUSNESS IN THE DAY THAT HE SINNETH. WHEN I SHALL SAY TO THE RIGHTEOUS, THAT HE SHALL SURELY LIVE; IF HE TRUST TO HIS OWN RIGHTEOUSNESS, AND COMMIT INIQUITY, ALL HIS RIGHTEOUSNESSES SHALL NOT BE REMEMBERED; BUT FOR HIS INIQUITY THAT HE HATH COMMITTED, HE SHALL DIE FOR IT.** Again, when I say unto the wicked, Thou shalt surely die; if he turn from his sin, and do that which is lawful and right; If the wicked restore the pledge, give again that he had robbed, walk in the statutes of life, without committing iniquity; he shall surely live, he shall not die. None of his sins that he hath committed shall be mentioned unto him: he hath done that which is lawful and right; he shall surely live. Yet the children of thy people say, The way of the Lord is not equal:

but as for them, their way is not equal. When the righteous turneth from his righteousness, and committeth iniquity, he shall even die thereby. But if the wicked turn from his wickedness, and do that which is lawful and right, he shall live thereby. Yet ye say, The way of the Lord is not equal. O ye house of Israel, I will judge you every one after his ways. (Ezekiel 33:12-20)

It is clear to see that a righteous person cannot rely on previous righteous if he commits sin. If I have driven for 50 years without ever breaking the speed limit, would that do me any good when I break it and get caught? Will it help me to say that I've gone 50 years without breaking the law? Will that clear me for when I do break it? Of course not. All those years of living within the laws of the land will not benefit me when I do break a law. God says the same thing is true with living our spiritual life. All our previous good is forgotten when we sin, but God goes further than the law of our land. He promises us that all of our previous sins will not be remembered when we start doing good and obeying Him. Our legal system keeps our "sins" on their books but God wipes them out. "As far as the east is from the west, so far hath He removed our transgressions from us" (Psalm 103:12).

Now, some people don't like these verses in Ezekiel because it condemns them in their sinful lifestyle, so they try to say that these verses refer to a **physical** death but not a **spiritual** death. Such an explanation is totally unwarranted for if this refers to a physical death, then those who do not sin will live forever here on earth. Also, there would be no chance for the righteous to sin and then repent, because they would die physically as soon as they sinned and there would be no opportunity for them to repent, yet these verses clearly tell us that the righteous person who does commit sin can repent and live again. The only possible death this passage is referring to is a SPIRITUAL death. Of course, this fits with all the other clear Scriptural references that have already been listed. God's ways are equal. It's man ways that are unequal—especially when they try to change the Scriptures to fit their preconceived ideas.

JESUS SPEAKS

No less an authority than Jesus Himself gave an illustration in Matthew 18:23-34:

> Therefore is the kingdom of heaven likened unto a certain king, which would take account of his servants. And when he had begun to reckon, one was brought unto him, which owed him ten thousand talents. But forasmuch as he had not to pay, his lord commanded him to be sold, and his wife, and children, and all that he had, and payment to be made. The servant therefore fell down, and worshipped him, saying, Lord, have patience with me, and I will pay thee all. Then the lord of that servant was moved with compassion, and loosed him, and **forgave him the debt.** But the same servant went out, and found one of his fellowservants, which owed him an hundred pence: and he laid hands on him, and took him by the throat, saying, Pay me that thou owest. And his fellowservant fell down at his feet, and besought him, saying, Have patience with me, and I will pay thee all. And he would not: but went and cast him into prison, till he should pay the debt. So when his fellowservants saw what was done, they were very sorry, and came and told unto their lord all that was done. Then his lord, after that he had called him, said unto him, O thou wicked servant, **I forgave thee all that debt**, because thou desiredst me: Shouldest not thou also have had compassion on thy fellowservant, even as I had pity on thee? And **his lord was wroth,** and delivered him to the tormentors, till **he should pay all that was due unto him.**

Let's notice a few significant points from this lesson. There was a servant who owed a very large debt and could not pay, so he fell at his Master's feet and worshipped him and asked for mercy. The Lord, having compassion on him, "forgave him the debt." This same servant then went to one of his servants and demanded that he pay a very small debt that was owed him. His servant begged for mercy but he refused to show any and put him in prison. It was then told the first servant's Master what had happened and the Master called him to give an account. He called this servant "wicked" and said: "I forgave thee all that debt, because thou desiredst me," but because of his sin of unforgiveness, the Master demanded that the **debt that was forgiven** now be paid in full. Verse 35 then says: **"So *LIKEWISE* shall My heavenly Father do also unto you,** if ye from your hearts forgive not every one his brother their trespasses." Our sin debt can be forgiven but IF we don't forgive others, the debt can be **reinstated!**

IN HIS PRESENCE

As already mention, Lucifer was perfect in all his ways **until** he committed sin and fell. John 8:44 tells us: Ye are of your father the devil, and the lusts of your father ye will do. **He was a murderer from the beginning, and abode not in the truth, because there is no truth in him.** When he speaketh a lie, he speaketh of his own: for he is a liar, and the father of it." Even though Lucifer was perfect, he **ABODE** not in the truth, so all his perfection is forgotten and Jesus said that he was a murderer **from the beginning.** This is what will happen on judgment day. Look at Matthew 7:21-23:

> "Not every one that saith unto Me, Lord, Lord, shall enter into the kingdom of heaven; but he that **doeth the will of My Father** which is in heaven. **Many** will say to Me in that day, Lord, Lord, **have we not**

**prophesied in Thy name? and in Thy name have
cast out devils? and in Thy name done many wonderful works?** And then will I profess unto them, **I never
knew you: depart from Me, ye that work iniquity.**

This is what Judas will hear when he stands before God.
He prophesied in Christ's name. He cast our devils. He healed
and did many wonderful works—yet God will say: "I never
knew you." **"All his righteousness that he hath done shall
not be mentioned"** (Ezekiel 18:24). In Luke 13:24-28 Jesus
says:

> **Strive** to enter in at the strait gate: for many, I
> say unto you, will seek to enter in, and shall not be
> able. When once the master of the house is risen up,
> and hath shut to the door, and ye begin to stand without,
> and to knock at the door, saying, Lord, Lord, open
> unto us; and he shall answer and say unto you, **I know
> you not** whence ye are: Then shall ye begin to say, **We
> have eaten and drunk in Thy presence, and Thou
> hast taught in our streets.** But he shall say, I tell
> you, **I know you not whence ye are; depart from
> Me, all ye workers of iniquity.** There shall be weeping
> and gnashing of teeth, when ye shall see Abraham, and
> Isaac, and Jacob, and all the prophets, in the kingdom
> of God, and you yourselves thrust out.

Notice that this passage says "I know you not." The people
to whom Jesus says this will respond that they were **IN HIS
PRESENCE** but He will still say: "I know you not...depart
from Me, all ye workers of iniquity."

After explaining about the judgment in Matthew 7, Jesus
then added:

> Therefore whosoever heareth these sayings of
> mine, and **doeth them,** I will liken him unto a wise

man, which built his house upon a rock: And the rain descended, and the floods came, and the winds blew, and beat upon that house; and it fell not: for it was founded upon a rock. And every one that heareth these sayings of Mine, and **doeth them not,** shall be likened unto a foolish man, which built his house upon the sand: And the rain descended, and the floods came, and the winds blew, and beat upon that house; and it fell: and great was the fall of it. (Matthew 7:24-27)

Notice that "doeth" ends with "eth." As mentioned earlier, this is the Greek present tense which means an **ONGOING** or **CONTINUAL PROCESS.** Verse 21 also has the word "doeth." The only ones who get to heaven are those who continually do God's will.

WISE AND FOOLISH VIRGINS

Let's look at Matthew 25:1-12. In this chapter Jesus gives us the example of the ten virgins. He said that five were wise and five were foolish. The foolish took no oil with them but the wise had extra oil.

And at midnight there was a cry made, Behold, the bridegroom cometh; go ye out to meet Him. Then all those virgins arose, and trimmed their lamps. And the foolish said unto the wise, Give us of your oil; for our lamps are gone out. But the wise answered, saying, Not so; lest there be not enough for us and you: but go ye rather to them that sell, and buy for yourselves. And while they went to buy, the bridegroom came; and **they that were ready went in with Him** to the **marriage: and the door was shut.** Afterward came also the other virgins, saying, Lord, Lord, open to us. But He answered and said, Verily I say unto you, **I know you not.**

Notice that all ten were virgins (representing purity) and they all had lamps. The problem was that some of them didn't have extra oil. The oil could be likened to bearing fruit. Since no fruit was borne, even though the person was a virgin and had a lamp, she was not ready to meet the bridegroom and when He came, He said "I know you not." We are then admonished in the very next verse: "Watch therefore, for ye know neither the day nor the hour wherein the Son of man cometh" (Matthew 25:13). **WE NEED TO BE READY, WAITING, WATCHING, AND DOING THE WILL OF THE LORD IF WE EXPECT TO GET TO HEAVEN.**

THE TALENTS

Jesus, in the next section in this same chapter, now gives a story of the talents. A master "called **HIS OWN SERVANTS**" and gave them varying amounts of commodities. One servant received five talents, another servant two talents, and yet another servant one talent. The person with five talents was able to increase the amount to ten talents and the person with two talents was able to turn it into four talents. However, the other servant with one talent went and hid it. When the Master returned, he asked each of them to give an account of what they did with their commodities.

And so he that had received five talents came and brought other five talents, saying, Lord, thou deliveredst unto me five talents: behold, I have gained beside them five talents more. His lord said unto him, Well done, thou good and faithful servant: thou hast been faithful over a few things, I will make thee ruler over many things: enter thou into the joy of thy lord. He also that had received two talents came and said, Lord, thou deliveredst unto me two talents: behold, I have gained two other talents beside them. His lord said unto him, Well done, good and faithful servant;

thou hast been faithful over a few things, I will make thee ruler over many things: enter thou into the joy of thy lord. Then he which had received the one talent came and said, Lord, I knew thee that thou art an hard man, reaping where thou hast not sown, and gathering where thou hast not strawed: And I was afraid, and went and hid thy talent in the earth: lo, there thou hast that is thine. His lord answered and said unto him, Thou **wicked and slothful servant,** thou knewest that I reap where I sowed not, and gather where I have not strawed: Thou oughtest therefore to have put my money to the exchangers, and then at my coming I should have received mine own with usury. **Take therefore the talent from him, and give it unto him which hath ten talents.** For unto every one that hath shall be given, and he shall have abundance: but from him that hath not shall be taken away even that which he hath. And **cast ye the <u>unprofitable servant</u> into outer darkness: there shall be weeping and gnashing of teeth.** (Matthew 25:16-30; See also Luke 19:12-26.)

Again, we need to notice a few points. All of these people were **servants** of the same Master. All of them received a commodity to work with. All of them had the same amount (or more) when the Lord returned for them, but the servant who **did nothing with his talent** was severely rebuked. <u>He still had what was given unto him</u> but he did not bear any fruit and Jesus told us in John 15:8 "Herein is My Father glorified, that ye **bear much fruit; <u>so</u> shall ye be My disciples.**" "Every branch in Me that **beareth not fruit He taketh away:** and every branch that beareth fruit, He purgeth it, that it may bring forth more fruit" (John 15:2). This is what happened to this servant. He did not bear fruit and therefore he was called "wicked," "slothful," and "unprofitable," and he was **cast into outer darkness.** "The way of the slothful man is as an hedge of thorns: but the way of the righteous is made plain" (Proverbs 15:19).

A CLOSE WALK

The parables of the ten virgins and the talents should make each one of us stop and think that the Christian walk is a close walk. The five foolish virgins still had their lamps and the slothful servant still had the talent that was given him, but none of them bore fruit and added to what was already given. This shows us that not only sins of commission can cause us to lose out spiritually, but also sins of omission. We need to **GROW** in grace. Peter says: "Ye therefore, beloved, seeing ye know these things before, beware lest ye also, being led away with the error of the wicked, **fall from your own stedfastness.** But **grow in grace,** and in the knowledge of our Lord and Saviour Jesus Christ" (II Peter 3:17-18a).

Another example of getting saved but not growing in grace could be taken from Matthew 12:43-45:

> When the unclean spirit is gone out of a man, he walketh through dry places, seeking rest, and findeth none. Then he saith, I will return into my house from whence I came out; and when he is come, he findeth it empty, swept, and garnished. Then goeth he, and taketh with himself seven other spirits more wicked than himself, and they enter in and dwell there: and the last state of that man is worse than the first. Even so shall it be also unto this wicked generation.

This person got all cleaned up—his house was "garnished" (beautiful, adorned, decorated, embellished) and "swept"—but it was also "empty." He was not growing in grace and because of an empty house, evil spirits entered into him again and he was worse off than before. "Wherefore laying aside all malice,

and all guile, and hypocrisies, and envies, and all evil speakings,
As newborn babes, desire the sincere milk of the word, that
YE MAY GROW thereby: If so be ye have tasted that the
Lord is gracious" (I Peter 2:1-3).

Chapter Eleven

SINNING EVERY DAY IN THOUGHT, WORD, AND DEED

Many people say: "I sin every day in thought, word, and deed." After covering all the previous issues, can you still possibly think that we can sin <u>every</u> day and still be pleasing in God's sight?

I John 3:6-10 reveals:

> Whosoever abideth in Him **SINNETH NOT:** <u>whosoever sinneth hath not seen Him</u>, neither known Him. Little children, **LET NO MAN DECEIVE YOU:** *he that doeth righteousness is righteous,* even as He is righteous. **HE THAT COMMITTETH SIN IS OF THE DEVIL;** for the devil sinneth from the beginning. For this purpose the Son of God was manifested, that He might destroy the works of the devil. **WHOSO- EVER IS BORN OF GOD DOTH NOT COMMIT SIN;** for his seed remaineth in him: and he cannot sin, because he is born of God. <u>In this</u> the children of God are manifest, and the children of the devil: **whosoever doeth not righteousness is not of God,** neither he that loveth not his brother.

Trying to explain away verse 8, someone said that only a person who commits **HABITUAL** sin is of the devil. I ask you: "Isn't committing sin **EVERY DAY** habitual? What is more habitual than a DAILY routine? So, even while trying to justify a sinning lifestyle, one is condemned by the Bible. Besides, a person who is habitually honest, but has stolen just one time is still a thief. A person who tells the truth most of the time but on occasion tells a few lies, is still a liar. A person who murders only one person is a murderer. Likewise, if a person lives a holy life as a practice, but commits a few occasional sins, he is a sinner and will remain thus until he confesses it, regardless of whether or not he was once saved!

I John 5:18 says: "We know that whosoever is born of God **SINNETH NOT;** but **he that is begotten of God keepeth himself,** and that wicked one toucheth him not.**" Notice the word "keepeth" ends in "eth" and is therefore a continual process that we are to engage in. Once again we can see the security of the believer **AS LONG AS** we obey Christ's command. **IF** we keep ourselves, Satan cannot touch us and no one can pluck us out of the Father's hand.

Here are just a few more verses for you to ponder.

✤ **"Whoso keepeth the commandment shall feel no evil thing:** and a wise man's heart discerneth both time and judgment" (Ecclesiastes 8:5).

✤ "Thou wilt keep him in perfect peace, whose mind is stayed on Thee: because he trusteth in Thee" (Isaiah 26:3).

✤ "Righteousness keepeth him that is upright in the way: but wickedness overthroweth the sinner" (Proverbs 13:6).

✤ "Verily, verily, I say unto you, If a man keep My saying, he shall never see death" (John 8:51).

✤ **"He that keepeth the commandment keepeth his own soul; but he that despiseth His ways shall die"** (Proverbs 19:16).

✲ "And hereby we do know that we know Him, IF we keep His commandments" (I John 2:3).

✲ Jesus said: "Why callest thou Me good? there is none good but one, that is, God: but **IF THOU WILT ENTER IN-TO LIFE, KEEP THE COMMANDMENTS**" (Matthew 19:17).

✲ "Blessed are they that hear the word of God, **and keep it"** (Luke 11:28).

✲ "But the mercy of the Lord is from everlasting to everlasting upon them that fear him, and His righteousness unto children's children; **To such as** keep **His covenant, and to those that remember His commandments to** do **them"** (Psalm 103:17-18).

✲ "He that hath My commandments, and **keepeth them,** he it is that loveth Me: and he that loveth Me shall be loved of My Father, and I will love him, and will manifest Myself to him" (John 14:21).

✲ "He that loveth Me not keepeth not My sayings: and the word which ye hear is not Mine, but the Father's which sent Me" (John 14:24).

✲ "Jesus answered and said unto him, If a man love Me, he will keep My words: and My Father will love him, and We will come unto him, and make Our abode with him" (John 14:23).

✲ "Lay hands suddenly on no man, neither be partaker of other men's sins: **keep thyself pure"** (I Timothy 5:22).

✲ "If ye love Me, keep My commandments" (John 14:15).

✲ "Here is the patience of the saints: here are they that **keep the commandments of God**, and the faith of Jesus" (Revelation 14:12).

❧ "For this is the love of God, that we keep His commandments: and **His commandments are not grievous"** (I John 5:3).

❧ "Blessed are they that keep His testimonies, and that seek Him with the whole heart" (Psalm 119:2).

❧ "By which also ye are saved, **IF** ye keep in memory what I preached unto you, <u>unless ye have believed in vain</u>" (I Corinthians 15:2).

❧ "That thou keep this commandment **without spot, unrebukeable, <u>until the appearing of our Lord Jesus Christ</u>"** (I Timothy 6:14).

❧ **"If ye keep My commandments, ye shall abide in My love;** <u>even as I have kept My Father's commandments</u>, and abide in His love" (John 15:10).

❧ **"Blessed** are they that keep judgment, and he that **DOETH RIGHTEOUSNESS AT ALL TIMES"** (Psalm 106:3).

❧ "He that saith, I know Him, and keepeth not His commandments, **is a liar,** and the truth is not in him. But whoso **keepeth His word, in him verily is the love of God perfected:** <u>hereby</u> know we that we are in Him" (I John 2:4-5). We know that we are in Christ <u>if</u> we are <u>keeping</u> His commandments.

❧ "And he that **keepeth His commandments dwelleth in Him,** and He in him. And **<u>hereby</u> we know that He abideth in us,** by the Spirit which He hath given us" (I John 3:24).

❧ "All the paths of the Lord are mercy and truth <u>unto such as **keep** His covenant and His testimonies</u>" (Psalm 25:10).

❧ "Let us hear the conclusion of the whole matter: Fear God, and <u>keep His commandments</u>: for this is the whole duty of man" (Ecclesiastes 12:13).

There is no way that we can continue to commit willful sin and still be a child of God. One popular author wrote: "Is there a Christian here who has not sinned to-day? Is it not a fact that every one of us sins in thought, or word, or in deed, probably every day of our lives?" Is this true? Of course not. My Bible tells me in I John 2:1: "My little children, these things write I unto you that **YE SIN NOT.**" The word "sin" is in the aorist tense in Greek. The aorist tense is a one time situation, like when Jesus died, it was recorded in the aorist tense. In other words, John is saying that we are not to sin even <u>one</u> time, but **IF** (not **WHEN**) we do sin, then we have an advocate: "If any man sin, we have an advocate with the Father, Jesus Christ the righteous" (I John 2:1b). However, Jesus does not forgive unconfessed sin and if we fail to confess our sins, then He will not forgive us. Paul also tells the Ephesians: "But fornication, and **ALL UNCLEANNESS,** or covetousness, **LET IT NOT BE <u>ONCE</u> NAMED AMONG YOU, as becometh saints."**

The Christian walk is more than not PRACTICING sin. It is living a HOLY life. Besides, if I committed a sin every day in thought, word, and deed, would you believe that that would add up to over 1,000 sins **PER YEAR!** What a far cry from the **holy life** we are commanded to live. Paul himself said: "Ye are witnesses, and God also, how holily and justly and unblameably we behaved ourselves among you that believe" (I Thessalonians 2:10). No sinful living for Paul and he even had witnesses he could call on to prove it!

A CROWN OF LIFE

We do, however, need to have a proper definition of sin. I John 3:4 gives it: **"Whosoever committeth sin transgresseth also the law: for SIN IS THE TRANSGRESSION OF THE LAW."** John is not talking here about a mistake but a **willful and conscious sin.** He also says: **"All unrighteousness is** sin" (I John 5:17). Human frailties, weaknesses, and mistakes are not sins. The Bible clearly bears this out. Hebrews 10:26: "For if we **SIN WILFULLY.**" Number 15:30: "But the soul that doeth ought PRESUMPTUOUSLY...the same reproacheth the Lord; and that soul shall be cut off from among his people." (See also Deuteronomy 1:43; 17:12-13.) The Psalmist said in Psalm 19:13: "Keep back Thy servant also from PRESUMPTU-OUS sins; let them not have dominion over me: then shall I be upright, and I shall be innocent from the great transgression." There is a difference between a PRESUMPTUOUS or WILL-FUL SIN and a sin through ignorance. One is intentional and the other is done without the person's knowledge of it at the time. (See Leviticus 4:2, 13, 22, 27; 5:15, 18; Numbers 15:24-29; Acts 3:17; 17:30; I Peter 1:14; II Peter 2:10; Ephesians 4:18.)

When Jesus healed the man on the sabbath day, He told him: "Behold, thou art made whole: **SIN NO MORE, LEST A WORSE THING COME UNTO THEE**" (John 5:14). There are two things that need to be pointed out here. If this man had to sin every day, then he was far worse off **AFTER** meeting Jesus than before meeting Him. Also, did Jesus give an **IMPOSSIBLE** command? Did He tell this man to do something that Jesus knew he could not do? Of course not! Since it was possible for this man to **SIN NO MORE,** it is also possible for **us** to live without sin.

This does not mean that you won't ever again be tempted to sin. But when you are tempted, you don't have to yield. "Know ye not, that to whom ye yield yourselves servants to obey, his servants ye are to whom ye obey; **whether** of sin unto death, **or** of obedience unto righteousness?" (Romans 6:16).

Satan even tempted Jesus to commit sin but He did not succumb to the temptation. I Corinthians 10:13 tells us: "There hath no temptation taken you but such as is common to man: but **God is faithful,** who will not suffer you to be tempted above that ye are able; **but will with the temptation also make a way to escape,** that ye may be able to bear it." When a temptation comes, a way of escape is also provided. It is up to us, however, to choose the way of escape or to yield to the temptation and commit sin. "Blessed is the man that <u>endureth</u> temptation: for when he is tried, he shall receive the crown of life, which the Lord hath promised to them that love Him" (James 1:12).

Prayer is the best antidote there is against temptation: "Watch ye and pray, that ye enter not into temptation: The spirit indeed is willing, but the flesh is weak" (Matthew 26:41; Mark 14:38; See also Luke 22:40, 46).

Living without sin, however, does not mean living without mistakes, but there is a BIG DIFFERENCE between a willful sin and a mistake. Part of our problem today is that we do not have a Biblical definition of sin. It is obvious that a mistake and a sin are different because Jesus told this man he would be worse off if he sinned. Now if a mistake and a sin are the same thing, this man was in a sad condition, but "SIN is the TRANS-GRESSION of God's law" (I John 3:4). On the other hand, a mistake is not a WILLFUL TRANSGRESSION.

Jesus also told the woman taken in adultery: "Neither do I condemn thee: go, and <u>SIN NO MORE</u>" (John 8:11). If Jesus told these people to "GO AND **SIN NO MORE**," then it is also possible for us to not commit willful sin.

Whosoever abideth in Him SINNETH NOT: whosoever sinneth hath not seen Him, neither known Him. Little children, let no man deceive you: he that DOETH righteousness is righteous, even as He is righteous. He that committeth sin is of the devil; for the devil sinneth from the beginning. <u>For this purpose the Son of God was manifested</u>, that He might destroy

the works of the devil. WHOSOEVER IS BORN OF
GOD DOTH NOT COMMIT SIN....In this the children
of God are manifest, and the children of the devil:
whosoever doeth not righteousness is not of God,
neither he that loveth not his brother. (I John 3:6-10)

BE YE HOLY

"That ye may be sincere and **WITHOUT OFFENCE
TILL the day of Christ**" (Philippians 1:10). "That He might
present it to Himself a glorious church, NOT HAVING SPOT,
OR WRINKLE, OR ANY SUCH THING; but that it should
be **HOLY AND WITHOUT BLEMISH**" (Ephesians 5:27).
In fact, the purpose of Christ's birth was to save His people
FROM their sins: "thou shalt call His name JESUS: for **He
shall save His people FROM THEIR SINS**" (Matthew
1:21). Titus 2:14: "Who gave Himself for us, that He might
REDEEM US FROM ALL INIQUITY, and **PURIFY** unto
Himself a peculiar people, zealous of good works." Romans
12:1: "I beseech you therefore, brethren, by the mercies of
God, that ye present your bodies a living sacrifice, **HOLY,
acceptable unto God,** which is your reasonable service."

Ephesians 1:4: "He hath chosen us in Him before the
foundation of the world, that we should be **HOLY AND
WITHOUT BLAME before Him** in love." "That ye may be
blameless and harmless, the sons of God, **without rebuke**, in
the midst of a crooked and perverse nation, among whom ye
shine as lights in the world" (Philippians 2:15). "Wherefore,
beloved, seeing that ye look for such things, be diligent that ye
may be found of Him in peace, **without spot, and blameless**"
(II Peter 3:14).

Colossians 1:22: "To present you **HOLY AND UN-
BLAMEABLE AND UNREPROVEABLE in His sight.**"
I Peter 1:16 (and Leviticus 11:44): **"Be ye holy; for I am**

holy." I John 2:6: "He that saith he abideth in Him ought himself also so to walk, EVEN as He walked." How did Jesus walk? Hebrews 7:26 answers this: "For such an high priest became us, who is HOLY, harmless, UNDEFILED, SEPARATE FROM SINNERS, and made higher than the heavens." These verses and many, many more like them, leave NO ROOM for the Christian to sin every day in thought, word, and deed!

Richard S. Taylor states:

> The proper Christian attitude toward sin is one of abhorrence. If a Christian insists on calling everything sin, he will either lose this proper attitude toward sin, or live in a state of condemnation and darkness. Neither alternative is scriptural....Moreover, if he actually makes no distinction between sins of ignorance and sins of choice, will he not be apt to manifest the same deadly carelessness toward one as the other? Will this not lead to antinomianism? Thus do we see that in the very nature of the case an unreasonably broad definition creates a tendency toward a loose attitude.

> The Christian also becomes involved in a contradiction of the Word of God. He insists on a definition of sin which gives the lie to every verse that commands and promises a righteous life. If we can properly call the shortcomings resulting from human infirmity true sins, it becomes evident that true righteousness in this life is but a dream. We cannot be sinning and living a holy life at once. Thus, when we read that we may serve God 'in holiness and righteousness before him *all* the days of our *life*' (Luke 1:74, 75), this definition of sin cries, "Impossible!"

Someone else has it explained it like this: "Sinlessness does not mean that we are not able to sin, but that, thank God, we are able not to sin."

THE GNOSTICS

When John wrote his Gospels, there was a prevalent theory circulating called Dualism or Gnostism. The Gnostics taught that the spirit was perfectly holy but the material aspect or the body was evil and could not be made holy. They taught that even though a person was sensual, a drunkard, licentious, a murderer, etc., that the spirit itself was still holy because the body and the spirit are two separate entities. They therefore denied the need for the atonement of Christ and claimed that they were without sin (even though they were committing vile sins). They believed that they did not need to be cleansed from sin because they thought the spirit was righteous. To counteract this false notion, John wrote: "If we say that we have no sin, we deceive ourselves, and the truth is not in us" (I John 1:8). This verse is very applicable to many so-called "sinning Christians" because they believe that even though they are sinning they are still righteous before God and cannot lose their salvation. These people are our modern-day Gnostics. John said that if we believe in this false doctrine "We **deceive** ourselves, and **the truth is not in us.**"

Those who have an unbiblical definition of sin may think they are "sinning" in some areas where they really are not. If we have a Biblical definition of sin, all the Scriptures fall into place and there is **NO** contradiction, but if we have an incorrect definition of sin, then we make the Bible to be full of impossible and impractical commands and demands—as well as making it impossible to go to heaven. I believe a lot of our misunderstanding focuses on this very issue of the <u>definition</u> of sin. Also, a big issue is how much we really love God. If we TRULY love Him with our whole heart, then we will not want to hurt or displease Him in ANY way. This attitude alone will keep us from committing willful sins. I John 5:3: "For this is the love of God, that we keep His commandments: and **His commandments ARE NOT GRIEVOUS.**" He has not given commandments that are hard to keep. Jesus Himself said: "Take my yoke upon you, and learn of Me; for I am meek and lowly in heart: and ye shall find rest unto your souls. For **MY YOKE IS EASY, AND MY BURDEN IS LIGHT**" (Matthew 11:29-30). He is not asking us to do the impossible—or even the extremely difficult. His demand is reasonable and possible. "If ye love Me, keep My commandments" (John 14:15). "**IF** ye keep My commandments, ye shall abide in My love; <u>even as I have kept My Father's commandments,</u> and abide in His love" (John 15:10).

Let's look at more Scriptures as this is our only guide. For instance, not all anger is sinful. In fact, we are told in Ephesians 4:26: "Be ye angry, and SIN NOT." In other words, there is an anger that is righteous ("righteous indignation"). Jesus Himself was angry when He saw the people making His Father's house "a den of thieves" (Matthew 21:13; Mark 11:17; Luke 19:46), yet "in Him is NO sin" (I John 3:5). Psalms 7:11 tells us that "God is angry with the wicked every day." There are many places in the Bible that show God's anger and wrath. He was angry with Moses (Deuteronomy 1:37; 4:21); with Israel (Deuteronomy 9:8; II Kings 17:18); with Aaron (Deuteronomy 9:20); with Solomon (I Kings 11:9); etc.

God is jealous: "For thou shalt worship no other god: for the Lord, whose name is Jealous, is a jealous God" (Exodus 34:14; Exodus 20:5; Deuteronomy 4:24; 5:9; 6:15; Joshua 24:19; Joel 2:18).

Jesus was troubled in His spirit (John 11:33; 12:27; 13:21). God became wearied with mankind: "My spirit shall not always strive with man" (Genesis 6:3). "Ye have wearied the Lord with your words. Yet ye say, Wherein have we wearied Him? When ye say, Every one that doeth evil is good in the sight of the Lord, and He delighteth in them; or, Where is the God of judgment?" (Malachi 2:17).

Jesus seemed to be harsh when He called the Pharisees some names: "O generation of vipers, how can ye, being evil, speak good things? for out of the abundance of the heart the mouth speaketh." (Matthew 12:24). Matthew 23:33: "Ye serpents, ye generation of vipers, how can ye escape the damnation of hell?" Matthew 23:13: "But woe unto you, scribes and Pharisees, hypocrites! for ye shut up the kingdom of heaven against men: for ye neither go in yourselves, neither suffer ye them that are entering to go in." (See also Matthew 23:14, 15, 23, 25, 27, 29; Mark 7:6; Luke 12:56.) When Jesus was hungry and found a fig tree without fruit, He condemned it (Matthew 11:12-14). Obviously, then, not every emotional outburst is sin, although, if taken to an extreme, it can be sin—or, at least, can lead to sin. For example, Hebrews 12:15 warns us about bitterness: "Lest any root of bitterness springing up trouble you, and thereby many be <u>defiled</u>."

CAN MAN BE PERFECT?

In the list of sins that keeps one out of heaven, I do not see despair, self-pity, worry, impatience, etc., listed. The Bible clearly enumerates the sins that will keep one out of heaven in a number of places.

But fornication, and all uncleanness, or covetousness, let it not be once named among you, as becometh saints; Neither filthiness, nor foolish talking, nor jesting, which are not convenient: but rather giving of thanks. For this ye know, that no whoremonger, nor unclean person, nor covetous man, who is an idolater, hath any inheritance in the kingdom of Christ and of God. Let no man deceive you with vain words: for because of these things cometh the wrath of God upon the children of disobedience. (Ephesians 5:3-6)

Now the works of the flesh are manifest, which are these; Adultery, fornication, uncleanness, lasciviousness, Idolatry, witchcraft, hatred, variance, emulations, wrath, strife, seditions, heresies, Envyings, murders, drunkenness, revellings, and such like: of the which I tell you before, as I have also told you in time past, that they which do such things shall not inherit the kingdom of God. (Galatians 5:19-21)

But the fearful, and unbelieving, and the abominable, and murderers, and whoremongers, and sorcerers, and idolaters, and all liars, shall have their part in the lake which burneth with fire and brimstone: which is the second death. (Revelation 22:14-15)

Blessed are they that do His commandments, that they may have right to the tree of life, and may enter in through the gates into the city. For without are dogs, and sorcerers, and whoremongers, and murderers, and idolaters, and whosoever loveth and maketh a lie. (Revelation 21:8)

To say we can sin and still go to heaven is definitely unscriptural. Now, you can **try** to live in a false security if you want to, but we will **ALL** be judged by God's Word and when I stand before the throne of God, I do not want to hear: "I never knew you: depart from Me, ye that work iniquity" (Matthew 7:23b; See also Matthew 25:41; Luke 13:27). I want to hear: "Well done, good and faithful servant...enter thou into the joy of thy Lord" (Matthew 25:23).

NOTHING unclean can enter heaven. "And there shall in no wise enter into it any thing that defileth, neither whatsoever worketh abomination, or maketh a lie: but they which are written in the Lamb's book of life" (Revelation 21:27). "He that is unjust, let him be unjust still: and he which is filthy, let him be filthy still:

and he that is righteous, let him be righteous still: and he that is holy, let him be holy still" (Revelation 22:11).

PERFECT BEFORE GOD

Many teach that no one can be perfect or blameless in God's sight. But turning again to the Bible we can find several perfect people. Genesis 6:9 "These are the generations of Noah: Noah was a JUST MAN AND **PERFECT** in his generations, and Noah walked with God." Hezekiah said: "I beseech Thee, O Lord, remember now how I have walked before Thee in truth and with a **PERFECT HEART,** and have done that which is good in Thy sight" (II Kings 20:3; Isaiah 38:3). "The HEART OF ASA WAS **PERFECT** ALL HIS DAYS" (II Chronicles 15:17b).

"And the Lord said unto Satan, Hast thou considered My servant Job, that there is none like him in the earth, a **PERFECT** AND AN **UPRIGHT** MAN, one that feareth God, and escheweth evil? and still he holdeth fast his integrity, although thou movedst Me against him, to destroy him without cause" (Job 2:3; See also Job 1:8). The Lord Himself gave this description of Job, so we know that it is true.

Paul said: "Ye are witnesses, and God also, how HOLILY AND JUSTLY AND UNBLAMEABLY WE BEHAVED OURSELVES among you that believe" (I Thessalonians 2:10). Jesus Himself even said of Nathanael: "Behold an Israelite indeed, IN WHOM IS NO GUILE!" (John 1:47). "There was in the days of Herod, the king of Judaea, a certain priest named Zacharias, of the course of Abia: and his wife was of the daughters of Aaron, and her name was Elisabeth. And **they were both righteous** before God, **walking in all the commandments and** ordinances of the Lord **BLAMELESS"** (Luke 1:5-6).

In addition to these examples of perfect people, the Bible gives many commands for us to also be perfect and blameless. Consider the following: Matthew 5:48: **"BE YE THEREFORE PERFECT,** even as your Father which is in heaven is perfect." John 17:23: "I in them, and Thou in Me, that they MAY BE MADE **PERFECT** in one; and that the world may know that Thou hast sent Me, and hast loved them, as Thou hast loved Me." Philippians 2:15: "That ye may be **blameless** and harmless, the sons of God, without rebuke, **in the midst of a crooked and perverse nation,** among whom ye shine as lights in the world." I Timothy 3:2: "A bishop then must be **blameless,** the husband of one wife, vigilant, sober, of good behaviour, given to hospitality, apt to teach." (See also Titus 1:7.) I Timothy 3:10: "And let these also first be proved; then let them use the office of a deacon, being found **blameless."** I Timothy 5:7: "And these things give in charge, that they may be **blameless."** II Peter 3:14: "Wherefore, beloved, seeing that ye look for such things, **be diligent** that ye may be found of Him in peace, **without spot, and BLAMELESS."** Hebrews 12:14: "Follow peace with all men, and **holiness,** without which no man shall see the Lord" (Hebrews 12:14).

I Corinthians 2:6: "Howbeit we speak wisdom among THEM THAT ARE **PERFECT:** yet not the wisdom of this world, nor of the princes of this world, that come to nought." II Corinthians 13:11: **"BE PERFECT,** be of good comfort, be of one mind, live in peace; and the God of love and peace shall be with you." I Corinthians 1:8: "Who shall also confirm you unto the end, that ye may be **blameless** in the day of our Lord Jesus Christ." Philippians 3:15: "Let us therefore, AS MANY AS BE **PERFECT,** be thus minded: and if in any thing ye be otherwise minded, God shall reveal even this unto you." Colossians 1:28: "Whom we preach, warning every man, and teaching every man in all wisdom; that WE MAY PRESENT EVERY MAN **PERFECT** IN CHRIST JESUS." II Timothy

3:17: "That the MAN OF GOD MAY BE **PERFECT,** throughly furnished unto all good works." Hebrews 13:21: "MAKE YOU **PERFECT** in every good work to do His will, working in you that which is wellpleasing in His sight, through Jesus Christ." James 1:4: "But let patience have her perfect work, that YE MAY BE **PERFECT** AND ENTIRE, wanting nothing."

Genesis 17:1: "And when Abram was ninety years old and nine, the Lord appeared to Abram, and said unto him, I am the Almighty God; walk before Me, and BE THOU **PER-FECT.**" Deuteronomy 18:13: "THOU SHALT BE **PERFECT** with the Lord Thy God." Psalms 37:37: "Mark the **PERFECT** MAN, and behold the upright: for the end of that man is peace." I Peter 1:15-16: "But <u>AS</u> He which hath called you is holy, <u>SO</u> <u>BE YE HOLY</u> in all manner of conversation; Because it is written, **BE YE HOLY; FOR I AM HOLY.**"

A PROPER DEFINITION

Again, a proper definition of "perfection" is needed. Perfection does not mean never making a mistake, for if that were the case then the Scriptures are full of impossible commands. If the Bible is full of impossible commands, then the Bible cannot be trusted, relied upon or obeyed. If, however, **perfection means a perfect heart BEFORE GOD** (and not before man, for only God knows the motives and the intents of the heart—Hebrews 4:12), then we can live a perfect life— <u>just as the Bible commands us to do</u>. When God told Abraham to walk perfect He said that he was to walk perfect before God—not man or his wife or his neighbor (Genesis 17:1). This is not an angelic perfection nor is it an Adamic perfection but rather the perfection that comes from loving God and wanting to do His will and to please Him. A person with a truly cleansed heart wants the will of God to be done in his or her life.

A little girl may want to please her mother by bringing her a cup of tea, but on her way she may trip and spill the tea. Nonetheless, the intents of her heart were perfect, although by the **outward appearance** it may not appear to be so. **God looks on the heart** (I Sam. 16:7). At the same time, what is in the heart will eventually manifest itself in our lives. "For from within, out of the heart of men, proceed evil thoughts, adulteries, fornications, murders, Thefts, covetousness, wickedness, deceit, lasciviousness, an evil eye, blasphemy, pride, foolishness: All these evil things come from within, and defile the man" (Mark 7:21-23).

We are not to judge motives but we are to judge righteous judgment (John 7:24) and the Bible clearly tells us that if the tree is bearing rotten fruit, the tree itself is rotten (Matthew 7:17-18). If this same girl came in with a cup of tea and threw it on her mother, then we are able to judge by her actions that she wanted to be mean or to hurt her mother. We may not know the full motive behind her action, but we can easily see that her action was wrong. Now, sometimes Sis. A may think Bro. B is bragging but Bro. B may not have such an intention. This is where God must be the final judge, but if Bro. B goes out and commits murder or adultery, it is obvious that he is sinning for God's Word clearly tells us that murder and adultery are sins.

"Now unto Him that is **able to keep you from falling,** and to **present you faultless** before the presence of his glory with exceeding joy, To the only wise God our Saviour, be glory and majesty, dominion and power, both now and for ever" (Jude 1:24-25). "Finally, brethren, farewell. **Be perfect,** be of good comfort, be of one mind, live in peace; and the God of love and peace shall be with you" (II Corinthians 13:11).

Chapter Twelve

FOUR KINDS OF SOIL

Jesus gave a parable concerning four different types of soil representing various kinds of people who hear His Word and their reactions to it. Some people teach that the first three kinds of soil represent sinners and the fourth soil depicts the Christian. Is this what the Bible really teaches? To find out we need to check this parable in the Scriptures and see what the Bible plainly says without reading anything into it and without trying to reinterpret the clear meaning.

Turn to Luke 8:5-8 (see also Matthew 13:3-23 and Mark 4:3-20):

> A sower went out to sow his seed: and as he sowed, some fell by the way side; and it was trodden down, and the fowls of the air devoured it. And some fell upon a rock; and as soon as it was sprung up, it withered away, because it lacked moisture. And some fell among thorns; and the thorns sprang up with it, and choked it. And other fell on good ground, and sprang up, and bare fruit an hundredfold. And when He had said these things, He cried, He that hath ears to hear, let him hear.

These four verses could be open to different opinions concerning which soils represent the sinners and which ones represent the Christians, but there is no question as to the meaning of this parable when you look at Luke 8:9-15. Jesus' disciples didn't understand the parable and asked Him what it meant. He then plainly interpreted for them.

And His disciples asked Him, saying, What might this parable be? And He said, Unto you it is given to know the mysteries of the kingdom of God: but to others in parables; that seeing they might not see, and hearing they might not understand. Now the parable is this: **The seed is the word of God.** Those by the way side are they that hear; then cometh the **devil,** and **taketh away the word** out of their hearts, <u>lest they should believe and be saved</u>. They on the rock are they, which, when they hear, <u>receive the word</u> **with joy;** and these have no root, which **for a while BE-LIEVE,** and **in time of temptation** <u>FALL AWAY</u>. And that which fell among thorns are they, which, when they have heard, go forth, and **are** <u>choked</u> **with cares and riches and pleasures** of this life, and **bring no fruit to perfection.** But that on the good ground are they, which in an honest and good heart, **having heard the word,** <u>KEEP it,</u> *and* <u>bring forth fruit</u> **with pa-tience.**

Isn't it clear that only the first soil depicts a sinner and the other three soils are Christians? There are two kinds of these Christians who backslide and the third one continues on. Notice carefully that the seed (which is the Word of God—verse 11) that falls by the way side never takes root. The devil takes the Word from them "lest they should believe and be saved."

ROCKY SOIL

The next description is of the rocky soil where the Word is **RECEIVED** and **BELIEVED** <u>for a while</u> but there is no root. Mark 4:5-6 relates: "And some fell on stony ground, where it had not much earth; and immediately it sprang up, because it had no depth of earth: But when the sun was up, it was scorched; and because it had no root, it withered away." This seed did sprout but because there was no depth of earth, it **WITHERED AWAY.** There was life here <u>at one time</u>, but when persecution and tribulation came because of the Word, the person became offended and was unable to stand. He was not strong enough to endure tribulation and therefore he gave up. Matthew 13:20-21 explains: "But he that received the seed into stony places, the same is he that heareth the word, and anon with joy **receiveth** it; Yet hath he not root in himself, but **dureth for a while:** for when tribulation or persecution ariseth because of the word, by and by he is offended." Also, Luke 8:13: "And these are they likewise which are sown on stony ground; who, when they have heard the word, **immediately receive it with gladness;** And have no root in themselves, and so **endure but for a time:** <u>afterward,</u> when affliction or persecution ariseth for the word's sake, immediately they are offended." Is it any wonder that Mark 13:13 says: "Ye shall be hated of all men for My name's sake: but he that shall **endure unto the end, the same shall be saved."** (See also Matthew 24:13.)

The third illustration is with a thorny soil. Once again the Word is <u>received</u> but riches, cares, and pleasures **CHOKE** the Word and even though some fruit might be borne, it is not brought to perfection. John 15:2 reminds us: "Every branch in Me that beareth not fruit **He taketh away:** and every branch that beareth fruit, He purgeth it, that it may bring forth more fruit."

The last soil was good soil. Not only was the Word believed and received but it brought forth much fruit. John 15:8 states: "Herein is my Father glorified, that ye **bear much fruit;** so shall ye be My disciples." According to Matthew 13:8, 23 and Mark 4:8, 20, some soil produced thirtyfold, some sixtyfold, and some one hundredfold. Notice also that these people not only bring forth much fruit, they also **KEEP** the Word. Once again, this is the secret to being secure in Christ. <u>Keeping Christ's Word guarantees our security</u>. John 15:16 informs us: "Ye have not chosen Me, but I have chosen you, and ordained you, that ye should go and **bring forth fruit,** and that your fruit <u>**should remain:**</u> that whatsoever ye shall ask of the Father in My name, He may give it you."

Some fruit that a Christian needs to produce is listed in Galatians 5:22-24: "But the fruit of the Spirit is love, joy, peace, longsuffering, gentleness, goodness, faith, Meekness, temperance: against such there is no law. And **they that are Christ's have crucified the flesh with the affections and lusts."**

ONE WHO ERRS IS A SINNER

Let's move on to James 5:19-20: "Brethren, if any of you do err from the truth, and one convert him; Let him know, that he which converteth the sinner from the error of his way shall save a soul from death, and shall hide a multitude of sins." Notice that James is referring to "Brethren." It then says **IF** any of the brethren err (sin), and he be <u>**converted,**</u> that a **SINNER'S SOUL** was saved from **DEATH.** We **CANNOT** live in sin and remain a Christian and we will lose more than just our reward. The sinner's **SOUL** was saved from death.

Look also the illustration that Jesus Himself gave in Matthew 24:45-51 (See also Luke 12:43-48):

> Who then is a **faithful and wise servant,** whom his lord hath made ruler over his household, to give them meat in due season? **Blessed is that servant,** whom his lord when he cometh shall find so **doing.** Verily I say unto you, That he shall make him ruler over all his goods. <u>But and if</u> that **evil servant** shall

say in his heart, My lord delayeth his coming; And shall begin to smite his fellowservants, and to eat and drink with the drunken; The lord of that servant shall come in a day when he looketh not for him, and in an hour that he is not aware of, And shall cut him asunder, and **appoint him his portion with the hypocrites:** there shall be weeping and gnashing of teeth.

Observe that there is a "faithful and wise servant" who has been made lord over his master's household. He is called "blessed" **if** he is doing this when his master returns. However, if this **SAME** "faithful" servant who has been made ruler, begins to commit sin and is sinning when his master returns, he is called "evil" and will be cut asunder and receive the portion of hypocrites, and there will be "weeping and gnashing of teeth." This obviously is hell in light of Matthew 13:42, 50: "And shall cast them into a furnace of fire: there shall be wailing and gnashing of teeth." You see, this very **SAME** servant (who was **IN** the master's house and who was **FAITHFUL** enough to be receive a position of authority) can be called blessed or evil **DEPENDING** on his actions and conduct. An interesting comment is added to the story in Luke's gospel. It states:

And that servant, which knew his lord's will, and prepared not himself, **neither did according to his will,** shall be beaten with many stripes. But he that knew not, and did commit things worthy of stripes, shall be beaten with few stripes. For unto whomsoever much is given, of him shall be much required: and to whom men have committed much, of him they will ask the more. (Luke 12:47-48)

Remember, this is an illustration given by Jesus Himself. Why don't we just take what He says rather than what man says? Keep in mind Galatians 6:9 (and II Thessalonians 3:13): "Let us not be weary in well doing: for **IN DUE SEASON WE SHALL REAP, IF WE FAINT NOT.**

Chapter Thirteen

DO WE POSSESS ETERNAL LIFE NOW?

Does the believer possess eternal life at the present time? Yes, we do—to an extent. Since Christ is our eternal life (I John 5:11), if we are abiding in Him, we do have eternal life. But there are many verses that need to be looked at as well. Titus 1:1-2 says that Paul is "a servant of God, and an apostle of Jesus Christ....IN **HOPE OF ETERNAL LIFE.**" I Timothy 6:12 and 6:19: "Fight the good fight of faith, **LAY HOLD ON ETERNAL LIFE,** whereunto thou art also called, and hast professed a good profession before many witnesses....Laying up in store for themselves a good foundation against the time to come, that they **MAY LAY HOLD ON ETERNAL LIFE.**" "And HE THAT REAPETH RECEIVETH WAGES, AND **GATHERETH FRUIT <u>UNTO</u> LIFE ETERNAL:** that both he that soweth and he that reapeth may rejoice together" (John 4:36). "He that loveth his life shall lose it; and he that hateth his life in this world shall keep it <u>UNTO LIFE ETERNAL</u>" (John 12:25). "But now being made free from sin, and become servants to God, ye have your fruit unto holiness, and **the end everlasting life**" (Romans 6:22). "For bodily exercise profiteth little: but godliness is profitable unto all things, having promise of the <u>life that now is</u>, and of that <u>which is to come</u>" (I Timothy 4:8).

Jesus said: "There is no man that hath left house, or brethren, or sisters, or father, or mother, or wife, or children, or lands, for

My sake, and the gospel's, But he shall receive an hundredfold now in this time, houses, and brethren, and sisters, and mothers, and children, and lands, with persecutions; and **in the world to come eternal life**" (Mark 10:29-30). **"Keep yourselves in the love of God,** looking for the mercy of our Lord Jesus Christ **unto eternal life"** (Jude 1:21). "Labour not for the meat which perisheth, but for that meat which **endureth unto everlasting life,** which the Son of man shall give unto you: for Him hath God the Father sealed" (John 6:27). "That being justified by His grace, we should be made heirs according to the **hope of eternal life"** (Titus 3:7). "That by two immutable things, in which it was impossible for God to lie, we might have a strong consolation, who have fled for refuge to **lay hold upon the hope set before us"** (Hebrews 6:18). "To them who by **patient continuance in well doing** seek for glory and honour and immortality, **eternal life"** (Romans 2:7). "For ye have need of patience, that, **AFTER YE HAVE DONE THE WILL OF GOD, ye might receive the promise"** (Hebrews 10:36).

THE EARNEST PAYMENT

We do receive eternal life when we get saved, but this is just an **earnest payment** which can be forfeited. Ephesians 1:13 states: "In whom ye also trusted, after that ye heard the word of truth, the gospel of your salvation: in whom also after that ye believed, ye were sealed with that HOLY SPIRIT of promise, **WHICH IS THE EARNEST OF OUR INHERITANCE UNTIL THE REDEMPTION OF THE PURCHASED POSSESSION,** unto the praise of His glory." (See also II Corinthians 1:22 and 5:5.) What is the seal of God? "Nevertheless the foundation of God standeth sure, having **this seal,** The Lord knoweth them that are His. And, Let **EVERY ONE** that nameth the name of Christ **DEPART FROM INIQUITY"** (II Timothy 2:19). The seal of God is that we DEPART FROM INIQUITY. If we turn again to iniquity, the seal is broken.

Did you ever see a jar of preserves that had the seal broken? When some germ (or we could liken this to sin) is present, the seal is broken. That germ cannot remain in the preserves without breaking the seal. The same is true in our lives. If a root of bitterness or other sin springs up, we become defiled and the seal is broken. Also, this same Greek word for seal is used in several other passages such as in Matthew 27:66 where a seal was set on Christ's tomb but that seal was broken. Satan will be sealed for 1000 years but this seal will also be broken. The seals in Revelation will be broken. A holy life is required to keep the seal from being broken.

This seal (according to Ephesians 1:13) is just the **earnest payment**. When you go to purchase a home, you give a downpayment (earnest or security) on it. You now own that home for the time being. It's yours. You live in it and enjoy it and keep the payments up-to-date. However, if you fail to pay your 30 year mortgage payments after 28 years of trustworthiness, your home will be repossessed. It doesn't matter that you have paid faithfully all those years. All that counts is that you are **not now fulfilling** your part of the bargain. The home is then forfeited due to **your** lack of faithfulness to the commitment.

Of course, some people teach that if you are unfaithful, you just lose your crown. The crown of life, however, is the crown of ETERNAL LIFE. If I lost my crown of ETERNAL LIFE, I have lost my salvation. The Scriptures clearly reveal that Christ is our life and if I lose Christ, I've lost my eternal life. Colossians 3:4: "When **CHRIST, WHO IS OUR LIFE,** shall appear, then shall ye also appear with Him in glory." (See also I John 5:20.) By searching the Scriptures we can again see a contradiction in this type of theology. The Bible states that only those who **CONTINUE** to the end will receive this crown. Revelation 2:10: "Be thou **FAITHFUL UNTO DEATH,** and I will give thee a crown of life." Personally, I would rather believe what the Bible says than what man asserts.

Some will point to I Corinthians 3:14-15 to try to prove that a "sinning Christian" loses his rewards because his works will be burned up. (Of course, there is no such thing as a "sinning Christian." If there is a "sinning Christian" then there would also be "Christian sinners." How foolish to even subject something like this.) This passage in I Corinthians reads: "If any man's work abide which he hath built thereupon, he shall receive a reward. If any man's work shall be burned, he shall suffer loss: but **he himself** shall be saved; **yet so as by fire.**" If you read this portion of Scripture carefully, it says that the man's works will be burned up and he will be saved **"yet so as by fire."** In other words, he himself will also has to be put through the fire—not just his works. What also must be taken into consideration are the following two verses: "Know ye not that **ye are the temple of God,** and that **the Spirit of God dwelleth in you?** If any man **defile** the temple of God, **him shall God destroy;** for the temple of God is holy, which temple ye are" (I Corinthians 3:16-17). This is definitely referring to the possibility of Christian defiling the temple of God and being destroyed—not just his works.

HOW TO LOVE GOD

One must **ENDURE** before receiving the crown of life: "Blessed is the man that <u>endureth temptation</u>: for when he is tried, he <u>shall receive the crown of life</u>, which the Lord hath promised to them that love Him" (James 1:12). "Hearken, my beloved brethren, Hath not God chosen the poor of this world rich in faith, and heirs of the **kingdom** which He hath **promised to them that love Him?**" (James 2:5). How do we show our love for Christ? Here are a few verses:

✔ "For this is the love of God, that we keep His commandments: and His commandments are not grievous" (I John 5:3).

✔ "If ye love Me, keep My commandments" (John 14:15).

✔ "If a man love Me, he will keep My words: and My Father will love him, and We will come unto him, and make Our abode with him" (John 14:23).

✔ "He that hath My commandments, and **keepeth them,** he it is that loveth Me: and he that loveth Me shall be loved of My Father, and I will love him, and will manifest Myself to him" (John 14:21).

✔ "But whoso keepeth His word, in him verily is the love of God perfected: hereby know we that we are in Him" (I John 2:5).

✔ "He hath shewed thee, O man, what is good; and what doth the Lord require of thee, but to do justly, and to love mercy, and to walk humbly with thy God?" (Micah 6:8).

✔ "And we have known and believed the love that God hath to us. God is love; and he that dwelleth in love dwelleth in God, and God in him" (I John 4:16).

✔ "And this is love, that we walk after His commandments. This is the commandment, That, as ye have heard from the beginning, ye should walk in it" (II John 1:6).

✔ "If ye keep My commandments, ye shall abide in My love; even as I have kept My Father's commandments, and abide in His love" (John 15:10).

I don't live in fear of losing my salvation. **I am secure within the Father's hand.** On the other hand, I know that if I were to go out and steal, commit adultery, murder, etc., I would no longer be saved. I John 3:15 reveals that "NO murderer hath eternal life abiding in him." Paul repeatedly tells us that adulterers, thieves, etc., **CANNOT** enter heaven. Yes, there is forgiveness for them as I Corinthians 6:11 says: "SUCH **WERE** SOME OF YOU: but ye are washed, but ye are sanctified, but ye are justified in the name of the Lord Jesus, and by the Spirit of our God." If, however, these people remain in an unconfessed and unforgiven state, they cannot enter heaven—NO sin can enter heaven. I John 5:17 states: "ALL unrighteousness is sin" and I John 3:4 says: "Sin is the transgression of God's law." **"Therefore to him that knoweth to DO GOOD and doeth it not, to him it is sin"** (James 4:17), and "Sin when it is FINISHED bringeth forth death [spiritual or eternal death]." Of course, if we confess our sins, we can be forgiven again (I John 1:9).

AS LONG AS we are doing the will of God we have **NO WORRY** about salvation and we are **secure in Christ.** "He that DOETH the will of God ABIDETH FOREVER" (I John 2:17), and Christ is "the author of ETERNAL SALVATION unto all that OBEY Him" (Hebrews 5:9). We obey Him by keeping His commandments and "He that loveth Me not keepeth not My sayings" (John 14:24). **"His commandment IS life everlasting"** (John 12:50). "He that KEEPETH His commandments DWELLETH in Him and He in him" (I John 3:24). Notice "keepeth" and "dwelleth" end in "eth" which, as I've already explained, means a **CONTINUAL** process. AS we keep His commands, we continue to dwell in Him.

In Acts we find an interesting story. Although it does not directly pertain to our salvation, it shows an important point. When Paul was a prisoner for the cause of Christ, he was being sent to Italy for a trial. On the way there, the ship encountered strong winds and it looked as if there was no hope of being spared. In the midst of this trouble Paul spoke up and said: "I exhort you to be of good cheer: for there shall be **no loss of any man's life among you,** but of the ship. For there stood by me this night the angel of God, whose I am, and whom I serve, Saying, Fear not, Paul; thou must be brought before Caesar: and, lo, **God hath given thee all them that sail with**

thee." As they were nearing shore, some "shipmen were about to flee out of the ship." Now, <u>God had just promised</u> Paul that <u>no one's life would be lost</u>, but when the men were about to flee the ship, "Paul said to the centurion and to the soldiers, **Except these abide in the ship, ye cannot be saved"** (Acts 27:21-24, 30-31). The same is true spiritually. We are promised eternal life—but it is on the condition that we **abide in Christ.** If we leave our source of safety, then our eternal life is forfeited.

STAND FAST

Here are just a few more Scriptures that tell us that we must **CONTINUE** in the faith to be partakers of eternal life.

"For now we live, <u>if</u> ye **stand fast** in the Lord" (I Thessalonians 3:8).

"For we are <u>made partakers</u> of Christ, **IF WE HOLD THE BEGINNING OF OUR CONFIDENCE STEDFAST UNTO THE END"** (Hebrews 3:14).

➤ "Then said Jesus to those Jews which **BELIEVED** on Him, **IF ye CONTINUE in My word, THEN** are ye My disciples indeed" (John 8:31).

➤ "Now when the congregation was broken up, many of the Jews and religious proselytes followed Paul and Barnabas: who, speaking to them, **persuaded them to CONTINUE** in the grace of God" (Acts 13:43).

➤ "Confirming the souls of the disciples, and exhorting them to **CONTINUE in the faith,** and that we must through much tribulation enter into the kingdom of God" (Acts 14:22).

➤ "And you, that were sometime alienated and enemies in your mind by wicked works, yet now hath He reconciled In the body of His flesh through death, to **present you holy and**

unblameable and unreproveable in His sight: IF YE CON-TINUE in the faith grounded and settled, and be not moved away from the hope of the gospel, which ye have heard, and which was preached to every creature which is under heaven; whereof I Paul am made a minister" (Colossians 1:21-23).

➤ "That they might set their hope in God, and not forget the works of God, but **keep His commandments:** And might not be as their fathers, a stubborn and rebellious generation; a generation that set not their heart aright, and whose spirit **was not stedfast** with God....For their heart was not right with Him, neither were they stedfast in His covenant" (Psalm 78:7-8, 37).

➤ "Therefore, brethren, **STAND FAST,** and hold the traditions which ye have been taught, whether by word, or our epistle" (II Thessalonians 2:15).

➤ "Therefore, my brethren dearly beloved and longed for, my joy and crown, so **STAND FAST** in the Lord, my dearly beloved" (Philippians 4:1).

➤ "Therefore, my beloved brethren, **be ye stedfast, unmoveable,** always abounding in the work of the Lord, forasmuch as ye know that your labour is not in vain in the Lord" (I Corinthians 15:58).

➤ "Watch ye, **STAND FAST IN THE FAITH,** quit you like men, be strong" (I Corinthians 16:13).

➤ "Take heed unto thyself, and unto the doctrine; **CONTINUE IN THEM:** for in doing this thou shalt both save thyself, and them that hear thee" (I Timothy 4:16).

➤ "But **CONTINUE** thou in the things which thou hast learned and hast been assured of, knowing of whom thou hast learned them" (II Timothy 3:14).

➤ "And they **continued stedfastly** in the apostles' doctrine and fellowship, and in breaking of bread, and in prayers" (Acts 2:42).

➤ "And now, little children, **abide** in Him; that, when He shall appear, we may have confidence, and not be ashamed before Him at His coming" (I John 2:28).

➤ "He that saith he abideth in Him ought himself also so to walk, even as He walked" (I John 2:6).

➤ **"Whosoever abideth in Him sinneth not:** whosoever sinneth hath not seen Him, neither known Him" (I John 3:6).

Lord, who shall abide in Thy tabernacle? who shall dwell in Thy holy hill? **He that walketh uprightly, and worketh righteousness, and speaketh the truth in his heart.** He that backbiteth not with his tongue, nor doeth evil to his neighbour, nor taketh up a reproach against his neighbour. In whose eyes a vile person is contemned; but he honoureth them that fear the Lord. He that sweareth to his own hurt, and changeth not. He that putteth not out his money to usury, nor taketh reward against the innocent. **HE THAT DOETH THESE THINGS SHALL NEVER BE MOVED.** (Psalm 15:1-6)

KEEP UNSPOTTED FROM THE WORLD

"Let that therefore **abide** in you, which ye have heard from the beginning. **IF** that which ye have heard from the beginning **shall remain** in you, **ye** also **shall continue in the Son,** and in the Father. And this is the promise that He hath promised us, even eternal life" (I John 2:24-25). Notice here that the promise is eternal life but to obtain it you **must abide. If** you abide in Christ, **then** ye "shall continue in the Son." Consider also why John wrote this: These things have I written unto you concerning them that seduce you" (I John 2:26). There were false teachers in John's day as well as in our day who taught that the body could commit sin but that the spirit was still righteous, so John wrote this warning in order that these people would not be seduced and misled. Will **YOU** heed this warning?

Wherefore lay apart **all** filthiness and superfluity of naughtiness, and receive with meekness the engrafted word, which is able to save your souls. **But be ye doers of the word,** and not hearers only, <u>deceiving your own selves</u>. For if any be a hearer of the word, and not a doer, he is like unto a man beholding his natural face in a glass: For he beholdeth himself, and goeth his way, and straightway forgetteth what manner of man he was. But whoso looketh into the perfect law of liberty, and **CONTINUETH** therein, he being not a forgetful hearer, but a doer of the work, **this man shall be blessed** in his deed. If any man among you seem to be religious, and bridleth not his tongue, but deceiveth his own heart, this man's religion is vain. **PURE RELIGION AND UNDEFILED BEFORE GOD AND THE FATHER IS THIS,** To visit the fatherless and widows in their affliction, and **TO KEEP HIMSELF UNSPOTTED FROM THE WORLD.** (James 1:21-27)

Believing is not a once forever (Greek aorist tense) transaction. There is discipline and striving involved on our part. "Then said one unto Him, Lord, are there few that be saved? And He said unto them, **STRIVE** to enter in at the strait gate: for many, I say unto you, will seek to enter in, and shall not be able" (Luke 13:23). **"FIGHT THE GOOD FIGHT** of faith, <u>lay hold on eternal life</u>, whereunto thou art also called, and hast professed a good profession before many witnesses" (I Timothy 6:12). "Thou therefore endure hardness, as a good soldier of Jesus Christ. **No man that warreth entangleth himself with the affairs of this life; that he may please him who hath chosen him** to be a soldier. And if a man also strive for masteries, yet is he not crowned, <u>except he strive lawfully</u>" (II Timothy 2:3-5).

"Wherefore **we labour, that,** whether present or absent, **we may be accepted of Him"** (II Corinthians 5:9). "Let us **LABOUR** therefore to enter into rest, **LEST** any man **FALL** after the same example of unbelief" (Hebrews 4:11). "For we are **labourers** together with God: ye are God's husbandry, ye are God's building" (I Corinthians 3:9). "Now he that planteth and he that watereth are one: and every man shall receive his own reward <u>according</u> to his own labour" (I Corinthians 3:8). "Let us **HOLD FAST** our profession of faith **WITHOUT WAVERING"** (Hebrews 10:23). "**If** ye **CONTINUE** in the faith **GROUNDED AND SETTLED,** and **BE NOT MOVED AWAY** from the hope of the gospel" (Colossians 1:23). "For now we live, **IF** ye **STAND FAST** in the Lord" (I Thessalonians 3:7). "Let us not be weary in WELL DOING: for in due season we shall reap, **IF WE FAINT NOT"** (Galatians 6:9).

DON'T BE A CASTAWAY

Paul wrote in I Corinthians 9:24-27:

> Know ye not that they which run in a race run all, but one receiveth the prize? So run, that ye may obtain. And **every man that striveth for the mastery is temperate in all things.** Now they do it to obtain a corruptible crown; but we an incorruptible. I therefore so run, not as uncertainly; so fight I, not as one that beateth the air: But I keep under my body, and bring it into subjection: lest that by any means, when I have preached to others, **I MYSELF SHOULD BE A CAST-AWAY.**

Paul realized that he could strive in vain and lose out in the very end if he did not continue in the faith. Now, some claim that Paul would only lose his reward but the clear teaching of the Scripture is that Paul is referring to his salvation. He emphatically states: **"I MYSELF."** He uses a **DOUBLE** pronoun to let you know that he is referring to himself—not to some reward. Let's not read into the Scripture something that is not there.

Of course, at the end of Paul's life he wrote triumphantly: "For I am now ready to be offered, and the time of my departure is at hand. I have fought a good fight, I have finished my course, **I HAVE KEPT THE FAITH:** Henceforth there is laid up for me a crown of righteousness, which the Lord, the righteous judge, shall give me at that day: and not to me only, but unto all them also that love His appearing" (II Timothy 4:6).

In the Sermon on the Mount Jesus said: "For I say unto you, That except your righteousness shall **EXCEED** the righteousness of the scribes and Pharisees, YE SHALL **IN NO CASE** ENTER INTO THE KINGDOM OF HEAVEN" (Matthew 5:20).

As long as I do not sin, **I'm safe and secure in Christ.** Wouldn't you like to have the same assurance and security? You can, but you need to **OBEY** God's Word.

✦ "And as many as walk according to this rule, peace be on them, and mercy, and upon the Israel of God" (Galatians 6:16).

✦ "And the peace of God, which passeth all understanding, shall keep your hearts and minds through Christ Jesus" (Philippians 4:7).

✦ "God is our refuge and strength, a very present help in trouble" (Psalm 46:1).

✦ "Ye that love the Lord, hate evil: He preserveth the souls of His saints; He delivereth them out of the hand of the wicked" (Psalm 97:10).

✦ "We know that whosoever is born of God sinneth not; but he that is begotten of God keepeth himself, and that wicked one toucheth him not" (I John 5:18).

✦ "The Lord preserveth all them that love Him: but all the wicked will He destroy" (Psalm 145:20).

✦ "Wherefore the rather, brethren, give diligence to make your calling and election sure: for **IF** ye do these things, **ye shall never fall**" (II Peter 1:10).

✦ "Now unto Him that is **able to keep you from falling,** and to present you faultless before the presence of His glory with exceeding joy" (Jude 1:24).

Chapter Fourteen

THE CHOICE IS YOURS

This book has given hundreds upon hundreds of clear Bible references plainly showing that a Christian must walk holy before the Lord in order to be assured of heaven. God's plan has been laid out in His Word and now **the choice is yours.** Will you serve the Lord and obey His Word or will you turn to your own way and follow the lusts of the flesh? **Your eternal destiny hangs in the balance.** Don't be like the Israelites who continued on in their sin. "Yea, they turned back and tempted God, and limited the Holy One of Israel" (Psalm 78:41). "But if ye will not obey the voice of the Lord, but rebel against the commandment of the Lord, then shall the hand of the Lord be against you, as it was against your fathers" (I Samuel 12:15). "For rebellion is as the sin of witchcraft, and stubbornness is as iniquity and idolatry" (I Samuel 15:23).

"If it seem evil unto you to serve the Lord, **choose you this day whom ye will serve;** whether the gods which your fathers served that were on the other side of the flood, or the gods of the Amorites, in whose land ye dwell: **but as for me and my house, we will serve the Lord"** (Joshua 24:15). "I call heaven and earth to record this day against you, that I **have set before you life and death, blessing and cursing:** therefore **CHOOSE LIFE,** that both thou and thy seed may live: That thou mayest love the Lord thy God, and that thou mayest **obey** His voice, and that thou mayest **cleave unto**

Him: for **He is thy life,** and the length of thy days" (Deuteronomy 30:19-20a).

We today also limit God when we claim that we cannot live without sin. If you would turn your life fully over to Him, you'd be surprised at what He could do with and for you. All that we need to live righteously has been provided by God:

> According as His divine power hath given unto us all things that pertain unto life and godliness, through the knowledge of Him that hath called us to glory and virtue: Whereby are given unto us exceeding great and precious promises: that by these ye might be partakers of the divine nature, having escaped the corruption that is in the world through lust. And beside this, **giving all diligence, add to your faith** virtue; and to virtue knowledge; And to knowledge temperance; and to temperance patience; and to patience godliness; And to godliness brotherly kindness; and to brotherly kindness charity. For **if these things be in you, and abound,** they make you that **ye shall neither be barren nor unfruitful** in the knowledge of our Lord Jesus Christ....Wherefore the rather, brethren, **give diligence to make your calling and election sure:** *for if ye do these things, ye shall never fall.* (II Peter 1:3-8, 10)

If the Bible does not teach that a person can be saved and then fall away, it would be full of unnecessary verses and useless warnings. For example, take I Peter 5:8: "Be sober, be **vigilant;** because **your adversary the devil,** as a roaring lion, walketh about, **seeking whom he may devour."** The devil can't devour a sinner because he already has him and if a Christian is supposedly eternally secure, then he can't devour him either. Why, then, is this verse in the Bible? To whom is it addressed?

Of course, a close look at the context of this passage **CLEARLY** reveals that Peter is talking to the Christian.

Humble yourselves therefore under the mighty hand of God, that He may exalt you in due time: Casting all your care upon Him; for He careth for you. Be sober, be vigilant; because your adversary the devil, as a roaring lion, walketh about, seeking whom he may devour: Whom resist **stedfast in the faith,** knowing that the same afflictions are accomplished in your brethren that are in the world. But the God of all grace, Who hath **called us unto His eternal glory by Christ Jesus,** <u>after</u> that ye have suffered a while, **make you perfect, stablish, strengthen, settle you.** (I Peter 5:6-10)

Notice that this passage states that we have been called by God. It also refers to "brethren." It tells us that Satan is our adversary and we are to resist him as we remain **STEDFAST IN THE FAITH.** It also states that after we have suffered, we can be made **PERFECT** and be established and settled in Christ. There is **NO WAY** that this verse is written to the sinner.

EVERY WIND OF DOCTRINE

If you want to defend a sinning religion, you'll be able to find thousands of people to agree with you, but the majority is not always correct. In fact, the Bible warns that "<u>broad</u> is the way, that <u>leadeth to destruction</u>, and <u>many</u> there be which go in thereat" (Matthew 7:13) but "<u>strait</u> is the gate, and <u>narrow</u> is the way, <u>which leadeth unto life</u>, and <u>few</u> there be that find it" (Matthew 7:14).

If any man teach otherwise, and consent not to wholesome words, even the words of our Lord Jesus Christ, and to the doctrine which is according to godliness; He is proud, knowing nothing, but doting about questions and strifes of words, whereof cometh envy, strife, railings, evil surmisings, Perverse disputings of men of corrupt minds, and destitute of the truth...**from such withdraw thyself.** (I Timothy 6:3-5)

Paul states that we should "henceforth be no more children, tossed to and fro, and carried about with every wind of doctrine, by the sleight of men, and cunning craftiness, whereby they lie in wait to deceive." (Ephesians 4:14). If we study what the Bible says and do accordingly, we won't be constantly tossed to and fro and we won't be carried away with every doctrine that comes along. If we know the Bible, we'll be able to stand firm on certain issues and we won't be swayed by Bro. A's theory when he speaks and thereafter waver and go along with Bro. B's theory when we hear him. Rather, we will be able to say **"THUS SAITH THE LORD"** and if Bro. A's and/or Bro. B's views don't agree with the Bible, no matter how fluent and how persuasive they may be, we'll not fall for the "cunning craftiness" of men but will remain firm upon the Solid Rock, Christ Jesus.

I well remember one banking class I had taken. When the teacher asked a question I raised my hand and gave my answer. He then asked the rest of the class if anyone else had an answer. No one did, so he asked how many thought I was wrong and EVERYONE raised their hands. Since I had studied the lesson I KNEW I was correct but NOT ONE of the other students would agree with me. The teacher then told the class that I was correct and they were all wrong.

Now, what would have happened had I changed my mind and gone along with the majority? Would that have made me right because EVERYONE else thought they were correct? No, instead of ONE person being correct NO ONE would have been correct. In fact, had I gone along with the majority I would have been even more wrong than they were because I knew the truth and would have compromised what I had known to be right just to be accepted by the majority. But I stood firm and it paid off. What made the difference? I STUDIED the book and KNEW what I had studied and even though the ENTIRE class was in disagreement with me I could STAND FIRM on my answer. It was also a great feeling to hear the teacher say that I was right. This is one reason why Paul writes: **"STUDY** to show thyself approved unto God, a workman that needeth not to be ashamed, rightly dividing the word of truth" (II Timothy 2:15). We can stand firm even though most people will disagree with us and then one day we will hear our Master say "You were right, well done." So, by studying and knowing the Word of God (our lesson book) we will be better able to stand firm.

It doesn't matter if millions or even billions of people agree with you. The question is: Do **YOU** agree with God's Word? That is the deciding factor. Your eternal welfare is far too important to leave it in the hands of sinful men. John 8:32: "Ye shall know the truth, and the truth shall make you free." Jesus said: "I am the **way**, the **truth**, and the **life:** no man cometh unto the Father, but by Me" (John 14:6). He also prayed: "Sanctify them through Thy truth: Thy word is truth" (John 17:17). "He that doeth truth cometh to the light, that his deeds may be made manifest, that they are wrought in God" (John 3:21).

SEARCH THE SCRIPTURES

Moreover, "the wrath of God is revealed from heaven against all ungodliness and unrighteousness of men, who hold the truth in unrighteousness" (Romans 1:18) and "Who changed the truth of God into a lie" (Romans 1:25). When people refuse to hear the truth of God's Word they "shall be turned unto fables" (II Timothy 4:4). "This people draweth nigh unto Me with their mouth, and honoureth Me with their lips; but their heart is far from Me. But in vain they do worship Me, teaching for doctrines the commandments of men" (Matthew 15:8-9; Mark 7:6-7). "Having a form of godliness, but denying the power thereof: **from such turn away**" (II Timothy 3:5). I beg of you, please don't be turned unto the fable where you're told you can live a sinful life and still go to heaven. The Bible teaches that we must live a holy life to enter heaven. Let's not deny God's power to enable us to do what He commands us to do.

You may think you are getting by with a sinful life now but when you stand before a righteous and holy God on Judgment Day, what will your excuse be? If the verses given throughout this book were read in court and the Judge had to decide a case as to what the verses say, the Judge wouldn't be able to say: "It seems to mean..." or "I think it should read like this..." or "It can't possibly mean what it says...." He would be obligated to take the literal meaning of the verses. God is our Judge and Jesus is our Advocate (Lawyer) and when His Word is read in Court (Judgment Day), only the clear meaning of the Scriptures will be accepted. There won't be any room for opinions. It would be far better to accept His Word now and live by it, then to wait until Judgment Day to accept it when it will be too late. Remember: "He that is unjust, let him be unjust still: and he which is filthy, let him be filthy still" (Revelation 22:11a).

Let's say that I write out some specifications for a printer to print this book. I tell him that I want black ink on bright white paper. I explain that I want a full color cover with a glossy coating and I order 10,000 copies to be printed. When I receive the contract, I sign it and send the job in to be done. What would happen if he would use red ink on purple paper with a yellow and blue cover, print 6,000 copies? In addition to this, what if he would add his own comments to some areas and then delete some of what I wanted printed? I would break my contract with him. He can say that I promised him my job. He can also say that he did a printing job for me and that it took much effort and time and cost him a lot of money to use colored paper and colored ink, etc., but I can show him the contract and say that even though he printed the book at an expense to him, the **specifications** were changed and that the job is unacceptable. It really does matter if the terms are changed.

God, too, has laid down certain requirements in His Word and if we try to change them, we are only hurting and cheating ourselves—and **it still doesn't change the facts.** They will remain the same regardless of how hard one tries to change them.

In this book I have presented just **some** of the many, many Scriptures along this line. The Bible is full of **so many other verses that I could have listed,** but I feel that I've given enough for you to see what the Bible truly teaches. It is now time for you to **"SEARCH THE SCRIPTURES; for in them ye THINK ye have eternal life:** and they are they which testify of Me" (John 5:39). You will not be able to stand before a holy God and say that someone has never warned you. (Obviously, you didn't even need my book as warning since you already have God's Word.)

Right now you may even sincerely think you are okay, but sincerity IS NOT enough. You may sincerely go to your medicine cabinet and take out a bottle that you think is medicine but that is actually poison. Your sincerity will not stop you from the consequences. You could tell me to take a left turn, but I may sincerely think I was to take a right turn and go over a precipice. My sincerity is not enough.

Of course, there is no need for you to take a wrong turn. The Bible is God's road map to heaven and the path has been clearly marked out for us. All we have to do is follow His directions. We may change His road map and enjoy doing it and think everything will be fine, but when it comes time to make that final journey, we'll be on the wrong path. Changing His road map to make it fit our specifications won't do us any good in reaching our destination. Adding to God's Word and taking away from it is like changing His road map. The Bible warns: "If any man shall add unto these things, God shall add unto him the plagues that are written in this book: And if any man shall take away from the words of the book of this prophecy, **God shall take away his part out of the book of life, and out of the holy city,** and from the things which are written in this book" (Revelation 22:19).

After reading this book you may realize that you never were truly saved to begin with. If this is the case, why don't you decide **right now** that you will become a Christian and live a holy life. The first step is to be born again. John 3:3 emphasizes: **"EXCEPT** a man be born **AGAIN,** he **CANNOT** see the kingdom of God." How can one be born **AGAIN?** We all know that we were born once, our physical birth, but can we enter into our mother's womb and be born the second time (see John 3:1-17)? No. The second birth comes by being born into the family of God. John 3:16: "For God so **LOVED** the world [that includes **YOU!**] that He **GAVE** His only Begotten Son, that **WHOSOEVER** [that includes **YOU**] **BELIEVETH** [trusts, clings to, relies] on Him [God's Son, Jesus] should not perish [in hell], but have everlasting life."

God is a God of compassion and mercy. That's why He sent Jesus to die in our place so that we could go to heaven. He says: "Come unto Me, all ye that labour and are heavy laden, and **I will give you rest"** (Matthew 11:28). All you need to do is sincerely believe with all your heart that Jesus is the Son of God and to be willing to turn from your sins, whatever they are—big or small. Just "cast all your care upon Him; for He careth for you" (I Peter 5:7). Ask Jesus to come into your heart and help you to live for Him, and He **WILL** do it. "He that covereth his sins shall not prosper: but whoso **CONFESS-ETH AND FORSAKETH** them shall have mercy" (Proverbs 28:13). John 6:37 promises: "Him that cometh to Me I will **IN**

NO WISE cast out." Romans 10:9 states: "If thou shalt **CON-FESS** with thy mouth the Lord Jesus, and shalt **BELIEVE** in thine heart that God hath raised Him from the dead, thou **SHALT** be saved [born again]."

If you would like to be born again, pray your own prayer or sincerely pray the following:

Dear Jesus, I realize that I am a sinner. I believe that You died for my sins. Please forgive me of my past sins and come into my heart. Save me for Your sake, and help me to live for You. I ask this in Your name. Amen.

If you sincerely prayed and asked Jesus to forgive you of your sins, you will have the assurance that you are now a child of God. John 1:12 reveals: "But **AS MANY AS RECEIVED HIM,** to them gave He power to become the sons of God, even to them that **BELIEVE** on His name." Read your Bible **EVERY** day (start with the book of John), and find a Bible-believing church where you can worship God with other born again believers.

"Therefore being justified by faith, we have peace with God through our Lord Jesus Christ" (Romans 5:1), "and the peace of God, which passeth all understanding, shall keep your hearts and minds through Christ Jesus" (Philippians 4:7). "If the Son [Jesus Christ] therefore shall make you free, ye shall be free indeed" (John 8:36).

If you were saved at one time and now realize that you are backslidden, why don't you, too, determine to **repent** and follow Christ? Just confess your sins like Peter, Simon, David, and others. Pray like David prayed: **"Restore** unto me the joy of Thy salvation; and uphold me with Thy free spirit" (Psalm 51:12) and **"Create in me a clean heart,** O God; and **renew** a right spirit within me" (Psalm 51:10). You can now enjoy your security in Christ **AS** you walk in the light of His Word.

I may never meet you here on earth but I do trust to meet you in heaven as we gather around the throne of God. Until then let us serve the Lord with our whole being. "Thou shalt love the Lord thy God with all thy heart, and with all thy soul, and with all thy mind" (Matthew 22:37). "And the very God of peace sanctify you wholly; and I pray God your whole spirit and soul and body be **preserved blameless** unto the coming of our Lord Jesus Christ" (I Thessalonians 5:24). **"BLESSED ARE THEY THAT DO HIS COMMANDMENTS, THAT THEY MAY HAVE RIGHT TO THE TREE OF LIFE, AND MAY ENTER IN THROUGH THE GATES INTO THE CITY"** (Revelation 22:14).

SOME OTHER LITERATURE BY CATHY BURNS

BOOKS:

A One World Order Is Coming (116 pages)........................$ 5.95
Alcoholics Anonymous Unmasked (128 pages)...................$ 5.95
Hidden Secrets of Masonry (64 pages)..............................$ 4.95
Hidden Secrets of the Eastern Star (496 pages)..................$15.95
Mormonism, Masonry, and Godhood (132 pages)...............$ 6.95
Secure in Christ (136 pages)...$6.95

BOOKLETS: ....$0.50 each
Astrology and Your Future
Different Types of Friendship
Hidden Dangers of Reflexology
Hypnosis: Cure or Curse?
Questions and Answers About the New Age Movement
To Catholics with Love
What Is Your I.Q.?

ARTICLES:
Tongues and Related Issues (14 part series).......................$5.00
　　　　　1. Do All Speak in Tongues?
　　　　　2. Baptism in the Holy Ghost
　　　　　3. Sinful Lives and Tongues
　　　　　4. Signs and Wonders
　　　　　5. Prosperity and Riches
　　　　　6. The Power of Words
　　　　　7. Can We Create Our Own Reality?
　　　　　8. What Is Visualization?
　　　　　9. A Look at Inner Healing
　　　　　10. Are You a God?
　　　　　11. Misfits Removed!
　　　　　12. Renegades Excluded!
　　　　　13. Thy Kindgom Come!
　　　　　14. Will the Church Be Raptured?
Jay Gary: The Millennium Doctor.....................................$4.00

A Scriptural View of Hell (2 part series)...............................$1.00
Unholy Laughter? (2 part series)...$1.00

ARTICLES: ....**$ .50 each**
Chart Your Course with Orion International
Divination
Dowsing Is in the Bible!
I Have Sinned
Jason Winters and His Herbal Tea
March for Jesus (WHICH Jesus?)
New Age Love
Should We Name Names?
Some Occult Terms Explained
The Rapture—When Will It Occur?
Unity or D-i-v-i-s-i-o-n?
What Is Miscegenation?
Witchcraft in the Church
Ye Shall Not Surely Die

TRACTS: ....**$0.60 per dozen**
A Perfect Church (Malcolm Burns)
ABC's of Salvation
Divorce and Remarriage
I've Been Cheated! (Jean Burns)
My God Cannot Do Everything
Treasure of All Ages (Jean Burns)
What Are You Missing? (Jean Burns)
What Is Sin?

Please include postage for literature.
For orders, or a complete list of literature available, write to:

SHARING
212 East Seventh Street (C)
Mt. Carmel, PA 17851-2211

SHOCKING TRUTH REVEALED

HIDDEN SECRETS OF MASONRY

Dr. Cathy Burns

√ Does Masonry promote astrology and reincarnation?

√ Are Masonry and Christianity compatible?

√ What do the Masonic symbols represent?

√ Who is the **REAL** god of Masonry?

Discover hidden meanings, sexual overtones, the god they conceal, and much more. Fully documented with 276 footnotes.

64 pages • $4.95 (plus $1.25 postage) • ISBN 0-00-540512-2

Intriguing Mysteries Exposed!

♦ *Who founded the Eastern Star and **WHY**?*

♦ *Is it a secret society shrouded in obscurity?*

♦ *Is it compatible with Christianity?*

♦ *What is the meaning of the Cabalistic Motto?*

♦ ***WHO** is represented by the Star in the East?*

♦ *Is there a **GODDESS** connection?*

Over 100 pictures are included as well as 1453 footnotes, many taken directly from Eastern Star and Masonic sources.

This book takes you inside the Lodge room and on a journey through the five degrees. Secret passwords are revealed as well as the hidden meaning of symbols, colors, flowers, and gems, and the significance of the lambskin apron.

A special section is included on the *Rainbow Girls*.

For your gift of only $15.95 plus $1.55 shipping and handling.

496 pages • ISBN 0-00502-181-2

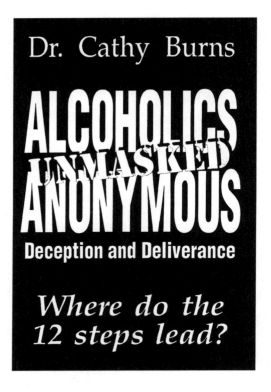

Dr. Cathy Burns

ALCOHOLICS UNMASKED ANONYMOUS

Deception and Deliverance

Where do the 12 steps lead?

- Who is the Higher Power of AA?
- Were AA's founders Christians or occultists?
- How is the New Age involved?
- How successful is AA's treatment program?
- Is alcoholism a sin or a disease?

Don't you think it's time to learn about Bill Wilson's adulterous affairs, LSD experimentation, as well as his and Dr. Bob Smith's interest in seances and spiritualism?

128 pages • $5.95 • ISBN 1-56043-449-X

A ONE WORLD ORDER IS COMING

"Peace, peace, we must have peace at any cost," is the cry being heard from every quarter today. If we don't soon agree to have a peaceful world, we may all die in a nuclear holocaust. So, what will it take to have a peaceful coexistence? The answer given is the establishment of a one world government. In addition to a one world government, there will be a one world religion and a one world economy. What is also needed in a one world government is a leader. Who will this leader be?

In spite of many plans for this one world government, there is still one obstacle in the way. What—or **WHO**—is this obstacle?

Each of these topics are discussed in detail in this book and then compared to the Bible to see how prophecy is being fulfilled.

For your gift of $5.95 plus $1.25 postage and handling.
116 pages • ISBN: 1-891117-00-9

Mormonism, Masonry, and Godhood

Dr. Cathy Burns

Can Angels Be Trusted?

The Church o f Jesus Christ of Latter-day Saints (Mormons) began on April 6, 1830. In this book Dr. Burns covers many of key Mormon doctrines as well as looking closely at Mormon's founder, Joseph Smith.

This well-documented book answers questions such as the following:

— What **talisman** was found on Joseph Smith when he died?
— Was Joseph Smith involved in **magical and occultic practices?**
— Is there a **Masonic connection?**
— What takes place inside the Mormon Temple?
— Was God once a man?
— Is **polygamy** necessary to attain heaven?
— How can a Mormon attain **godhood?**
— What does Mormonism teach about **baptism for the dead?**
— Was Jesus married?
— Was Jesus crucified because He was a polygamist?

132 pages • $6.95 plus $1.25 postage • ISBN: 1-891117-01-7